HELP!

MY FACEBOOK ADS SUCK
THIRD EDITION

By Malorie & Jill Cooper

eBook ISBN: 978-1-64365-096-8
Print ISBN: 978-1-64365-095-1

Cover Art by Malorie Cooper
Editing by Jen McDonnell, Bird's Eye Books

TABLE OF CONTENTS

FOREWORD

Hello, I'm Malorie, and together with my wife, Jill, and a few others who have joined our ranks, we're the Writing Wives.

We've been penning novels our whole lives, hoping against hope that we'd make it big. That dream stayed out of reach until 2016 when we mastered Facebook Ads.

That skill catapulted us into our full-time writing careers. We were finally living the dream.

Okay, it's not quite that simple, nor so cut and dried, but understanding ads and marketing did indeed get us to the point where we have made a comfortable living from writing for over six years.

A few years ago, I hit burnout (after writing over 100 books in 4 years) and was struggling to produce. I also had let my ad game slip. I considered going back to the regular working world, but the idea was just so…awful.

We were still well above six-figure authors, but without new releases, income was falling.

I was lamenting about this to some author friends, and most of them responded along the lines of, "We would kill to have what you consider a waning career! Teach us!"

Bolstered by that sentiment, Jill and I worked at restoring our ads to their former glory, and brought our income back up to where it needed to be.

Then we dove into teaching authors how to run Facebook ads profitably and with as little time consumed as possible.

To be fair, by this point (mid-2020), I had already written the first two editions of this book, spoken at numerous author conventions, and run a few webinars on mastering Facebook ads, but I'd never really made teaching and training a priority.

Oh, how that has changed.

Today, we have worked with hundreds of authors, helping them reach their goals—be it a comfortable supplementary income, or going full-time as author.

We've aided authors with their websites, launch plans, covers, taught how to research the market, worked through launch plans, and provided hundreds of hours of training and webinars as we've launched a successful (for both us and our clients) business of one-on-one coaching.

But during that time, Facebook ads changed *a lot*.

Over the past few years, the second edition of this book has become more and more outdated, and the time has finally come to rectify that!

That brings us to what you're about to read: a book that will not only take you through the process of creating ads, but teach you how to measure those ads and determine if they are working for you…and then scale them.

The Writing Wives,
Malorie & Jill Cooper
May the ads be ever in your favor.

MAKING YOUR OWN SUCCESS

> *Why do we think we have the chops to teach you about this subject?*

Before we begin, we want to talk a bit about what success looks like, and why we believe we're successful enough at Facebook ads to write a book about them.

As mentioned in the foreword, Facebook ads are the reason Jill and I are full-time writers today, and the reason our books have achieved bestseller ranks on Amazon multiple times and sold nearly two million copies.

We are neither the highest-earning authors out there, nor are we the best writers, but together, Jill and I have managed to reach income levels that far eclipse salaries I earned working as a software architect and CIO/CTO.

Our accomplishments come from testing, refining, and continuously improving our marketing strategies.

There are well over fifty thousand books coming out each month right now. You've got the storytelling part of the equation down, but no one will see your book unless you get it in front of them. Ads are an integral part of marketing your book, exposing it to the ever-increasing pool of readers.

The right marketing can give you a second stream of income, and perhaps even major success and the financial freedom that comes with it.

We manage tens of thousands of dollars in ad spend each month, for both our books and our clients'. We have a positive ROI on every ad that stays alive for more than three days, and we quickly identify ads that don't work, and kill them before they can soak up money.

Realizing your goals comes from knowing not only how to craft a good ad, but also how to spot a lemon and kill it—or figure out how to make lemonade. Continuous improvement requires you to set aside fear of increased spending on ads, which will be easier when you understand their performance and the return you'll get on that investment.

We believe that our success with Facebook ads (plus AMS, Pinterest, and Instagram ads) gives us the credibility to teach you how to profit with online advertising.

When we note a tactic that worked well for us, you can be assured that it netted hundreds or thousands of dollars in sales. Conversely, if we say that something did not work, or had only a mediocre return, you'll understand that just making our money back is not what we consider a win.

We sincerely hope that you don't take this as bragging. We only want you to know what success looks like so you can set achievable goals as you build up your own ad repertoire.

With that out of the way, let's get to it, and craft ads that work, while pruning the ones that do not.

Note, there is a glossary at the back of this book that explains many of the terms we'll use. If you're ever unsure about something, please reference it.

PART 1: KNOW YOUR READ-THROUGH

Part one of this book has nothing to do with ads. But if you don't read it and complete the spreadsheet linked at the end, you'll have no way to tell if your ads are profitable.

Exceptions are using your own spreadsheet for this, or using Author Helper (formerly Reader Links).

It's unwise to make an investment without being able to calculate the ROI (return on investment). If you don't know what your return is going to be, you don't know if you're sending good money after bad, flushing it all down the toilet.

In this section, we're going to discuss an example series of five books, and how to calculate the read-through (RT) of that series, and why this is *very important* when it comes to ads.

We're not suggesting that you can't run ads for books which are not in a series (either standalone, or loosely connected books), but those are much more difficult to calculate read-through for, and are therefore riskier.

This is mostly because our retailers (*read: Amazon*) do not give us the tools to know in what order our readers read our books. Without a linear series, it's very hard to tell how much total profit you will make from the sale of a given book. With a linear series, you can typically assume that readers start with book 1, and go in order to the end.

This being said, even un-ordered series (most often found in thriller or romance markets) can still have their read-through estimated by assuming most people start with book 1.

The benefit of a linear series versus standalone books is that you only have to advertise the first book; then you can run it as a loss leader to build your funnel—which is to say, you make up the cost of advertising book 1 via the sales of subsequent books in the series.

In a non-linear series, it's possible to advertise any book, and it may be worthwhile to determine which book sells the best with Facebook ads, and market that one specifically. Though, if you do this, it gets pretty tricky to calculate read-through rates.

Now, as defined in the glossary, your read-through is, quite simply, how many of your readers read through each book and then pick up the next. I generally use this term to describe both Kindle Unlimited reads and ebook sales (which I sometimes hear referred to as "sell-through").

There are two types of read-through: cumulative, and book over book.

CUMULATIVE READ-THROUGH (CRT)

What does cumulative read-through have to do with ads and ROI, anyway?

What we are trying to determine with cumulative read-through (CRT) is the value of a sale of book 1 in your series. In simple terms, you want to be able to say, "If I sell book 1 in my series, on average, I will see x dollars in royalties."

To do this, we need to know how many readers actually make it to the end of our hypothetical 5-book series, what books they drop off on, and how much we earn in royalties for each book (both on sales and KU reads).

This calculation is super simple for sales. At the end of the month, take all the sales of the last book in the series, and divide it by the sales of the first book in the series.

For example, if book 1 sold 876 copies, and book 5 sold 514 copies:

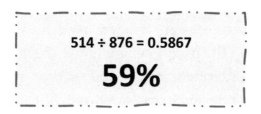

$$514 \div 876 = 0.5867$$

59%

This would mean that your entire series has a 59% RT. This is a pretty good read-through. Six years ago, it would have been mediocre, but with the volume of books being published as we roll into 2023, it's not bad at all.

To work out the net profits across the entire series, you need to do this for each book in the series (book x divided by book 1).

Don't panic. The end of Part 1 has a link to a spreadsheet that will do all this math for you. All you have to do is plug your monthly numbers into the sheet.

If you're in Kindle Unlimited (aka KDP Select), then this is a bit trickier.

NOTE: If you have an omnibus edition that encompasses books 1-3 (for example), or just released the last book in the series, you will see the later books sometimes have read-through of over 100%. If this is the case, you may be better off using your all-time sales numbers rather than monthly sales.

Another way to deal with omnibus editions is to add the sales number to each book it contains, but divide the KU reads between all three.

Example: If the books 1-3 omnibus had 10 sales and 12,000 page reads, add 10 sales to books 1, 2, and 3, but add only 4,000 page reads to each of those three books.

SIMPLE READ-THROUGH EXAMPLE

	Sales	Sales CRT	KU Reads	KU Reads CRT
Book 1	100		43000	
Book 2	65	65%	41000	95%
Book 3	50	50%	40500	94%
Book 4	48	48%	39800	93%
Book 5	45	45%	39000	90%

Cumulative Sales RT on the series: 45%
Cumulative KU Reads RT on the series: 90%

You'll notice that the KU RT is much higher than the sales RT. This mirrors real-world experience (mine, and that of many authors I've worked with). RT on KU is almost always in the 70% – 90% range, or higher.

In this hypothetical series, the first book is $0.99, and the subsequent four are $3.99. They have the following KENPC values: 451, 511, 614, 499, 457. KENPC is Kindle Edition Normalized Page Count, which is how many "pages" you will get paid for if a reader goes through the entire book.

For the example above, if we work out the diminishing cumulative read-through for both sales and reads, and assume a KENP rate of $0.0045, then for every sale of book 1, we make $5.94, while for every *borrow* of book 1, we make $10.27.

If your book has been picked up by KU readers and gained traction there, it is very common to see at least one borrow for every sale at a minimum. This means that a sale of your first book nets you $16.21, because every time you sell a book, you also get an average of one borrow.

The reason we have to estimate this is because Amazon gives us no insight into our borrow counts, and KU reads can take as long as 4-6 weeks to come in (because you have to wait for the reader to finish the book, not because Amazon's reporting is *that* bad).

In the linked spreadsheet, these numbers are calculated with the correct royalties and delivery fees, so that is what an actual book's royalties could look like, given the prices and page count stated (for U.S. sales only, as each country has its own KU page rate).

A FUN EXERCISE

Sometimes it's difficult to mentally convert the KU pages read into the number of books borrowed. If you get your KENPC for each book in your series, you can convert pages read to books read, and compare your read volume between KU and sales more accurately.

The spreadsheet linked at the end of Part 1 has a spot for your KENPC, and it will show you full books read if you fill it in.

On your KDP bookshelf, click the ... next to an eBook listing and choose "KDP Select Info" to see a book's KENPC.

This is displayed at the bottom of the "KDP Info" page for each book in your series.

To see how many full KU reads you've had, divide your monthly pages read for a book by that book's KENPC, and you'll have the full reads value.

> 43000 (pages read) ÷ 451 (KEPNC value)
> # = 95.34 full reads

Caveat: KU misses some reads, and not everyone reads to what the system considers to be the "end" of the book. Therefore, you may wish to take the number of KENPC in a book and reduce it by 5%.

> 451 (KENPC) x 0.95 (removes 5%) = 429
> 43000 (pages read) ÷ 429 (KEPNC value)
> # = 100.23 full reads

We reduce the book's page count by 5% because sometimes the KENPC includes the backmatter pages which may not get read.

Seeing your KU page reads as full books read and comparing them to sales can help you understand the value, or lack thereof, for your books in the program.

Book Report supports this as well. You can enable a column named "Borrows" that lists a converted value from KU pages read to an estimate of books read in KU.

On the settings page, set the KENPC full-read percent to about 95 to get a more accurate reading.

Set this lower if you have sample chapters for subsequent books.

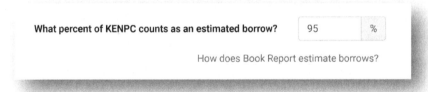

WARNING SIGNS

If your Sales RT for book 1 to book 2 is below 30%, something is wrong. If your KU book 1 to book 2 RT is below 60%, something is wrong.

By "wrong," I mean something has caused your readers to decide they don't want to carry on. Usually, this means something pissed them off; there's a problem with your writing, or you have a cliffhanger where the main conflict in the story is not resolved.

It can also mean that the book's backmatter isn't optimized in order to guide readers to the next book.

Expect to see very different RT values depending on price. If book 1 is 99c, or free, you will see much lower RT to book 2 (possibly as low as 20%). If it is full price (ie: the same as the rest of the books in the series), then you can expect a 40%+ RT from book 1 to book 2.

BOOK-OVER-BOOK (BOB) READ-THROUGH (RT)

This type of read-through is less important for ad ROI calculation, but I want to talk about it for a moment, nonetheless.

This is the RT between one book and the next. For example, if you have 45 sales in a given month on book 3 in your series, and 38 sales of book 4, you divide the later book's sales by the earlier book's sales to get your read-through percentage.

$$38 \div 45 = 0.84$$

84%

Therefore, the book-over-book read-through (BOB RT) between books 3 and 4 is 84%.

That would be a decent RT, but perhaps a bit on the low side this late in the series. Most of the time, folks see RT in the 90% – 95% range later in their series.

Here's an example of a healthy BOB RT:

> **Book 1 –> Book 2: 50% to 75%**
> **Book 2 –> Book 3: 80% to 95%**
> **Book 3 –> Book 4: 85% to 98%**
> **Book 4 –> Book 5: 90% to 100%**

If you see a particular book fall off a cliff in regards to BOB RT, then you know you've made a mistake. You probably killed off a beloved character and lost part of your readership.

Chances are, your book's reviews will tell you what you did wrong.

FINAL THOUGHTS ON CALCULATING KU READS

This was a fun little exercise on how to turn those arbitrary KENP "read" numbers into something more meaningful. It's also necessary for the next step; but fear not, this is all done by the simple spreadsheet I've provided.

Again, once you have the KENPC for each book, divide your number of page reads for the month by that value, and you'll have the number of "full reads" of that book.

Given a KENPC value of 514 for book 1, and a total pages-read of 45833, we would end up with:

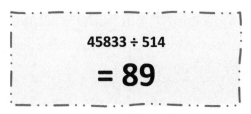

This means that 89.16 complete read-throughs of book 1 were made.

"Wait! You have no way of knowing that those page reads accounted for 89 full reads. It could have been 178 half-reads!"

If you had the reaction above, you're completely right in your thinking. We *don't* know this to be true—especially on book 1. However, we don't calculate CRT (cumulative read through) for book 1, so it doesn't really matter that much.

We do know, however, that anyone who reads book 2 likely read all of book 1, so when we calculate our CRT for book 2 and beyond, we'll still get a meaningful number.

Remember, for KU, we don't get paid by the full read, but rather, by each page read. Thus, for our net profit calculations, whether someone read the full book doesn't really matter; all that matters is the page-reads volume.

Converting KENP reads to full book numbers is handy because it can convey the value of KU to you, vis-à-vis how many books your readers are consuming in the program.

READ-THROUGH CALCULATOR SPREADSHEET

OK, math may not be your thing, and that was probably more than you wanted to do.

To make this simpler, and a bit more foolproof, I've created a spreadsheet where you can plug in all your sales numbers for a month, and it will give you your net profits per sale and per read.

You then can add your expected profits together, and divide that sum by how many clicks it takes to make a sale to arrive at your Cost per Click tolerance level.

This spreadsheet will allow you to calculate read-through in a series. There is one tab for a 5-book series, and another tab for a 10-book series. If your series doesn't have those exact numbers, simply pick the tab that applies best and input 0 for sales and reads for any books you don't have.

Also, if you have a permafree first book, put in 0 for the royalty rate.

Get it here:
https://bit.ly/3M0VQWR

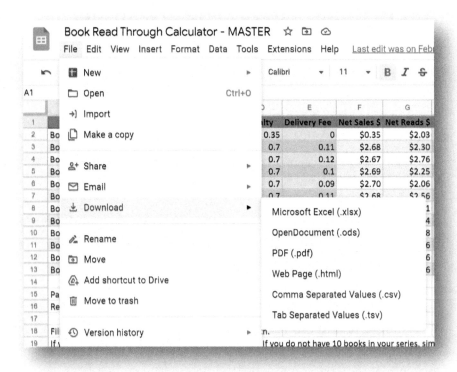

(You will need to save a copy or download the spreadsheet in order to make changes)

Alternatively, the Author Helper service now has a feature based on the above spreadsheet that will also calculate your read-through values.

APPLY READTHROUGH TO AMS ADS ACoS

While this book isn't about AMS ads, the math we do to determine the read-through royalties from follow-on books works for AMS as well.

Once the sheet is filled out, it knows the royalty rate of each book and can work out what profit you make at various ACoS levels.

This makes identifying profitable AMS ads very simple.

AMS	Cost of Sale	Sales Profit (no KU)	Reads Profit (KU incl)
500% ACoS	$ 4.95	$ 7.52	$ 29.70
400% ACoS	$ 3.96	$ 8.51	$ 30.69
300% ACoS	$ 2.97	$ 9.50	$ 31.68
200% ACoS	$ 1.98	$ 10.49	$ 32.67
100% ACoS	$ 0.99	$ 11.48	$ 33.66

The example series in the spreadsheet has pretty good KU reads, so those KU numbers are high, but it goes to show how profitable a 10-book series with good read-through can be.

PART 2: START WITH THE CREATIVE

If you've made ads before, you know that crafting the creative (images and ad copy) is the final step. However, that doesn't mean you should do it last.

Going through the mechanics of building an ad tends to activate the analytical portion of our brains and switch off the creative part. By the time most of us make it to the third section of ad creation, we're mentally wiped and will stick just about anything in there.

In my experience, it's best to make your creative ahead of time—and preferably not on the same day you make your ad.

ROCKING YOUR AD COPY (AKA PRIMER WORDS)

Priming has been used for ages in ads and is well known in psychology.

In a nutshell, words evoke feelings (positive, negative, and everything in between), and it's important to use the right words to elicit the right feelings.

"Why's that?" you ask? It's because...

99% of all purchase decisions are based on emotion.

Sorry to burst anyone's bubble, but we are rarely as analytical as we like to think we are.

Here's an example of an email an author may send to their readers. There's nothing inherently bad about this email—except that it uses negative priming words.

> Hey everyone,
>
> I've been working on the new book, but I've hit some setbacks. Mainly that Gerald won't cooperate with where I want the story to go. It's been a bit frustrating, but I'll get him in line. In the meantime, *Rising Star* got this really mean 1-star review and it's killing my sales, so I'm in a bit of a bad headspace.
>
> I'll keep you updated—the book is coming soon.

Some of the negative words in this email are: *setbacks, frustrating, really mean, killing, bad headspace.*

The author is being honest, but there's a way to word this email so that it leaves the reader with both positive feelings, and positive actions they can take.

Here's a different take on the same email:

> Hey folks,
>
> I've been plugging away on the next tale of the Chosen Saga and it's really coming together. Of course, Gerald won't cooperate with where I want the story to go, but when has he ever been easy to deal with? That's why we love him, right?

I did notice the other day that *Rising Star* got a 1-star from someone who really didn't connect with the book. I respect that, but I worry it may keep some people from joining us on the adventure. If you think the book deserves a 5-star, I'd love a review or rating to help it get in more readers' hands.

I'd better get back to it. Sarah can't keep Gerald in line on her own.

GENERAL PRIMER WORDS

...that elicit positive responses and have positive associations:

- Join
- Gather
- Union
- Assemble
- Unite
- Rally (behind)
- Meet

...that have empowering associations:

- Ascend
- Encourage
- Bold
- Daring
- Epic
- Conquer
- Triumph
- Brave
- Sassy

...that trigger curiosity (clutch for mystery writers):

- Delve (into)
- Tempting

- Secret
- Unusual
- Unique (use sparingly)
- Explore
- Experience
- Bizarre
- Unhinged
- Oddball
- Disquieting
- Discover
- Mystery

...have pleasurable associations:

- Enjoy
- Curl up
- Imagine
- Love
- Warm
- Adore

...that are a bit salesy, but still good:

- Essential
- Detailed
- Bestselling
- Entertained

GENRE-ORIENTED PRIMER WORDS

...that are great for action or adventure:

- Thrust (into)
- Deadly
- Headlong
- Rogue
- High stakes
- Hunt
- Duty
- Gritty
- Uncover
- Thrilling
- Action-packed
- Suspenseful
- Legendary
- Thrill-ride
- Perilous
- Swashbuckling
- Challenge
- Courageous

...that are essential (see what I did there?) for romance:

- Sexy
- Irresistible
- Turned upside down
- Sinfully
- Passion
- Burns/Burning
- Desires
- Temptation
- Fire
- Really stupid (as in whoops, I fell for him/her/them)
- Find it in his/her/their heart

- Captured
- Enrapturing
- Mesmerizing
- Sensual
- Evocative
- Tantalizing
- Provocative
- Breathtaking
- Heartwarming
- Emotional
- Enchanting
- Allure
- Seductive
- Unforgettable
- Compelling
- Dreamy
- Captivating
- Tender
- Irresistible

...that convey key science fiction/dystopian tropes:

- Colonize
- Explore
- Across the stars/galaxy/universe
- Starship
- Spaceship
- Space Fleet
- Fallen

Fantasy/Epic/Dark/Fantasy/Paranormal/Supernatural:

- World-building
- Engaging
- Dark magic

- Dark
- Urban magic
- Chosen one
- Sword
- Shield
- Paranormal
- Mystical
- Magical
- Portal
- Shifters
- Beyond the veil
- Forbidden
- Magical
- Shadows
- Mysterious
- Gritty
- Enchanting
- Mythical
- Otherworldly
- Spellbinding

Science Fiction/Dystopian:

- Colonize
- Explore
- Dyson Sphere
- Ringworld
- Starship
- Spaceship
- Galactic
- Galactic Fleet
- Faster than Light
- Across the stars
- Star Fleet

- Fallen
- Alien
- Spacefaring
- Space Exploration
- Colonization
- Interstellar
- Intergalactic
- Multiverse
- Cosmic
- Vast
- Richly detailed
- Bold
- Interdimensional
- Cyberpunk
- Cyborg
- Dystopian
- Utopian
- Post-Apocalyptic
- Otherworldly
- Interplanetary
- Futuristic
- Speculative
- Quantum
- Cybernetic
- Implants
- Robotics
- High-Tech
- Railgun
- Laser
- New Frontiers
- Final Frontier
- Tech noir

There are many, many more words that can be primers for your genres, but rather than list them all, I hope this will give you enough information to start looking at the blurbs/descriptions of books that are selling well in your genre to seek out the words they're using that are priming their readers the right way.

Finally, here is a list of words to *avoid*, as they have been shown to trigger negative reactions in people (due to overuse and salesyness):

- Groundbreaking
- Revolutionary
- Perfect
- Impossible
- Miracle
- Visionary
- Transformative
- Jaw-Dropping
- Spellbinding
- Game-changer
- Always
- Unimaginable
- Radical
- Fundamental
- Avante-Garde
- Life-Changing

A LOOK AT THE UX (User Experience)

There are two portions of ad copy: the "Primary Text" (for some people, this may only be labeled as "Text") and the "Headline".

People read web pages and web content in a relatively consistent pattern. Whether we naturally read content this way or have been trained to the pattern is a fun, nerdy debate, but what manifests the most is the "F/Z" pattern.

These patterns describe the way our eyes track across a screen and how we process the information. In traditional media, we tend to read in a Z pattern, but on the internet (especially on mobile devices), we read in the F pattern.

THE Z PATTERN

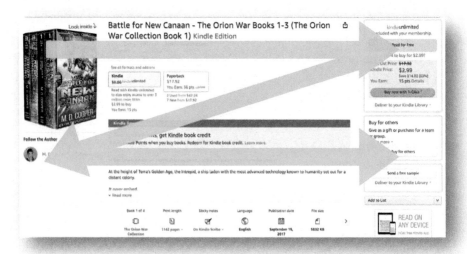

THE F PATTERN

There are, of course, some caveats to this. The first is that high-contrast images tend to catch our attention before text.

This is definitely prevalent when we're scrolling through social media. We've become very accustomed to skimming the text and pausing only when an image or video catches our attention.

THE SOCIAL MEDIA AD PATTERN

This is not universal for everyone. Some folks do read social media ads in an F, which means we need to structure our ads to work for both types of people.

Given that most people start with the image, you might think that we'd begin there, but it's important to work out what you're going to say, then to find the image(s) that complement the words.

WHAT'S IN A HEADLINE

This little stretch of text (which can only support 8-10 words) must do *a lot* of work.

It has to:

- give context to the image the reader saw first.
- reinforce that the ad is for a book.
- function as a CTA (call to action).
- work as a tagline for your book.

I'm probably missing something, but honestly, this is enough to juggle for now.

(BTW, the paragraph above is an example of negative priming. Let's try it again.)

This is a good set to begin with. Let's start crafting a headline that will get people clicking and buying.

If you are using an image that contains your book's cover (as in, the complete cover with all the text, whether in 2D or 3D), then one doesn't need to rely on the headline to reinforce that the ad is for a book as much as one does if the image does not (such as the image on the prior page).

Here are some headline examples. I'm going to try to get a primer word, genre, and a trope or two in each.

BOOK IN IMAGE

Curl up next to a warm fire with this beach romance

Discover what's in store for Sarah in the world of Pandora

Delve into the mystery of the ghost key

Join this unhinged adventure across the seven seas

NO BOOK IN IMAGE

Grab a glass of wine, you'll be reading this romance all night

Author A. Danvers does it again in her new psychological thriller

Experience the tale of Rapunzel like never before

A hot, steamy sci-fi romance that you'll be reading on your lunch break

You'll note that some of these headlines are a bit long, and will likely get cut off with an ellipsis, such as this:

...and that's a good thing.

Those three dots are a mystery all on their own, making the reader wonder what's next, getting them to turn the page, so to speak.

TAGLINE FORMAT

Another option for your headline is to use something like your blurb's tagline. This is generally only a good idea if the image you're using is a book cover, or if the tagline implies book/reading/etc...

If it's already clear that the ad is for a book, then one can use something like these:

> I'm done with Sol. The system is rotting, and I want out.

> In the distant future, an ancient ship reappears, setting the galaxy on a course for war.

STRAIGHT-UP SALESY

A final option is to be straight-up salesy with your ad copy. This is where you can pimp price, accolades, or availability.

> Available wherever good books are sold

> Read for free on Kindle Unlimited

On sale for the first time ever at $2.99!

Obviously, the first option is ideal for wide, and the second is a KU headline. One thing to watch out for is saying "KU" or using other author/publisher terms. For example, most readers aren't going to think "Kindle Unlimited" as quickly as authors, and very few will know what "wide" means to us.

Generally speaking, I don't mention price, because I'm afraid I'll forget that my ad says the book is on sale, and then I'll change the price in KDP. So do so at your own risk.

MASTERING PRIMARY TEXT

This is where the rubber meets the road. If your image and headline weren't enough to get someone to mash the Learn More/Download button on the ad, your Primary Text will have to sell them.

There are about as many ways to do Primary Text as there are words to construct it with, but it boils down to three main types: short, medium, and *long*.

SHORT AD COPY

Short Primary Text is structured much like a headline or tagline, but usually about twice the length, though ideally under two sentences.

This copy can take a number of forms. It can be your character saying something snarky in first person, it could be a snippet from an amazing review, it could be a tagline....

What it needs to be is something that grabs people's attention, doubles down on the genre or tropes that the image and headline conveys, but presents new mysteries and unknowns, leaving the reader wanting more.

Here are a few examples I whipped up. Don't agonize over these. Write them, let them sit for a day, then come back and tweak the wording. Analyzing the ad will tell you which are converting, and which can be consigned to the void.

> Kris thought she was ready for anything...but a freaking dragon is going too far!
>
> Love is supposed to be easy. Ask Jane and she'd tell you no greater lie had ever been told. Kurt intends to prove her wrong.
>
> A sword. In a stone. Kim would have laughed at how cliché it all was—if not for what happened next...

There are additional examples in later sections.

MEDIUM-LENGTH AD COPY

Medium-length ad copy is roughly as long as a blurb, in the 200 – 300 word length.

This can be similar a regular blurb (though don't just use the same blurb that's on your book) or it can be a couple of paragraphs pimping how awesome the book is and adding in great reviews. I've done ads that are straight dialogue, with the character talking to the reader, and salesy copy about a discount or special offer.

Look...I don't expect you to stop and read everything that shows up in your feed, but this is different.

You see...yesterday I turned into a dragon.

I know, I know...that's utterly ridiculous. Thirty hours ago I would have said the same thing, maybe even laughed a bit.

I'm not laughing now.

Not only did I turn into a dragon, but the entire city saw me—and now they're hunting for the "Great Terror of Trenton New Jersey."

FML. Seriously.

* * * * *

★★★★★ *This Is What a Space Opera Should Be*

★★★★★ *One of the absolute best in the Space Opera genre! Hands down M. D. Cooper doesn't disappoint!!*

★★★★★ *Off to a wonderful start! This space opera has it all*

★★★★★ *Fast-paced, readable military SF (with humans instead of cardboard cut-outs!)*

Join these Amazon reviewers and explore the world of Outsystem!

(To insert emojis, simply google the emoji name and copy/paste it into the ad. On windows hit the Win key and the . (period key) at the same time to bring up the emoji panel)

There are additional medium-length examples in later sections.

VERY LONG AD COPY

The third type is *very long* ad copy. In this scenario, one inserts the first chapter of the book (up to 2200 words) into the ad's Primary Text field.

If you choose to insert text from your book, be sure to add space between each paragraph, as it will paste in without any, and that will be very hard to read.

Here are some dos and don'ts:

- Do add space between paragraphs.
- Do check your text for any words that Facebook doesn't like (sex, sexy, ass, shit, hell, fuck, etc...).
- Do ensure that the chapter/scene ends on a strong hook.
- Don't include sex scenes.
- Don't include gore.

At the end of the excerpt, use this text:

Continue reading for free in Kindle Unlimited:
https://amazon.com/dp/ASIN
(where "ASIN" is the one for your ebook).

Or, if wide:

Continue reading on at your favorite retailer.
(followed by links to the various retailers—more on this in the next section).

CALL TO ACTION

Every good ad copy has a call to action (CTA). This can take a number of forms, but for our purposes, it's going to be a sentence prompting the user to click and buy/read.

Often, we see these in the style of "Read for free on Kindle Unlimited" or "Click and buy now!"

I prefer to be a little more subtle and focus on the emotional aspect of the book-buying/reading process.

For this, I go back to the primer words we talked about earlier. Here are some examples:

- Join Sarah on her epic adventure!
- For maximum reading pleasure, grab a glass of your favorite wine.
- Dive into this literary thrill ride!
- Help Peter navigate this unhinged fantasy adventure
- Crack this book open and help me save the Eastlands! (this could work if the ad copy is in first person).

Some of the above are a little more direct than others, but the key is to use primer words, be enticing, and let your voice shine through.

LINK YOUR TEXT

In the prior section, I showed how I add a link to the book following an excerpt from the book. However, I also add the links to my books at the bottom of the Primary Text, and I recommend you do as well.

I do this for a few reasons. The first is that it can't hurt to give people another place to click.

The second is that very often, I get comments in my ads asking if I have the book in print/audio/on a wide retailer.

I answer those questions when they are left on the ad, but I know there are potential readers who do not ask the question and simply move on.

This is what I put at the bottom of the Primary Text for a book enrolled in KU.

eBook: https://amazon.com/dp/ebook_ASIN
Print: https://amazon.com/dp/print_ASIN
Audiobook: https://amazon.com/dp/audiobook_ASIN
(if there is an audiobook version)

And if the book is wide:

Amazon: https://amazon.com/dp/ebook_ASIN
Apple: https://books.apple.com/us/book/BOOK_ID
B&N: https://barnesandnoble.com/w/BOOK_ID
Other Retailers: books2read/linktree/etc... link

Print: https://amazon.com/dp/print_ASIN
Audiobook: https://amazon.com/dp/audiobook_ASIN

You'll note that I've shortened all the links a bit by taking out the www on Amazon and B&N. I also removed the book title from inside the URL on all the links. The formats above will work for any book on those retailers to make tidier looking links.

BE DYNAMIC

Facebook supports the option to have more than one headline and text option per ad. If you click in the text field, a little "Add Option" button will appear.

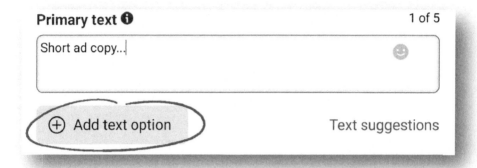

You might wonder why you'd want to provide more than one text option in the same ad, but the reason is simple. Facebook knows what sort of text is going to entice different people based on those folks' previous history of clicking on ads.

Primary text   3 of 5

Short ad copy...

Medium-length ad copy...   ✕

Long ad copy...   ✕

By giving Facebook options to work with, it can make a better ad for an individual human being that is more likely to get clicked on.

This is where our different types of headlines and Primary Text come into play. You don't have to pick just one (or make a separate ad for each); you can have your cake and eat it too, all in one ad!

Later, we'll get into how to assess those different text options to make sure they're all working.

THE PERFECT IMAGE

...does not exist. But the perfect image for an individual person? That just may be out there.

But before we get to that, let's talk about what should be in your image in broad strokes.

LET'S TALK BOOK COVERS

To use the book cover, or not to use the book cover, that is the question.

To answer this question, we need to travel back in time.

It's the year 2014. Facebook's ad platform launched seven years prior and is now a serious contender to Google's AdWords juggernaut.

In the past few years, Facebook has hit ad saturation. If they put more ads on their platform, people spend less time scrolling through their feed. But Facebook wants more money…what to do?

They can't jack up prices, because that will make them less competitive against Google. So they need to get more ads on the page.

The answer they came up with in years prior was to have ads look less like ads.

Facebook is a UGC (User Generated Content) platform, where the folks using it, you guessed it, make the content. And the content people make tends to be pictures of things like their cats and the latest meal they ate.

In short, back in 2014, UGC rarely ever had text on the images.

As a result, Facebook enforced a *No Text on Images* rule for ads, in an effort to make them look more like regular content and blend into people's feeds.

It worked, and they were able to up the ad density.

However, advertisers chafed at this, and it was an ongoing source of contention. Authors were particularly perturbed, because it meant that they couldn't use their book covers.

Fast forward to 2018. A change in user behavior has occurred in the past four years. Regular folk are more commonly posting images with text on them.

That's right: memes.

As a result, Facebook made a new rule. Ads could have text, but they couldn't have more than 20% of the image showing text.

How did they determine this percentage when looking at a given image? Poorly, that's how.

If an image had less than 20% text, it would get regular reach. If it had more, it would have its reach restricted.

This allowed a lot of authors to show their book covers if the text didn't take up too much room. It started to become common to show a scene with a 3D book cover on one side.

Advance to the end of 2020, and Facebook has decided that it can live with text on the images, so the 20% rule was removed. Theoretically, they no longer restrict ads in any way as a result of there being text on the image.

However, there is still an amount of throttling that takes place, in the form of user behavior.

Essentially, we're all pretty good at spotting ads and glossing over them. As a result, ads with a lot of text get clicked less, which means the CPC on those ads goes up, and they get shown less (because they burn through the budget faster).

So text on the ad image continues to hurt performance a bit. I test this a few times a year and it still holds true.

THE COUNTERARGUMENT

One of the things that retailers care about (Amazon especially) is your book's conversion rate on their site. This is the percentage of people who land on your book's details page *and buy*, out of the total number of visitors.

A healthy conversion percentage is 3-5%. A very good rate is 10%, while a poor rate is 1%.

That is to say, the best most people can reasonably hope for is a sale or borrow every 10 clicks, while the normal rate sits at something around one sale or borrow every 30-50 clicks.

If the conversion rate on your book is too low, you'll train Amazon's internal promotional systems to believe your book doesn't sell. This will de-prioritize your book and lower its placement in search results for more generalized terms, and it will decrease the number of people it sends release and *"you might be interested in"* emails to, amongst other side effects.

In a nutshell, low conversion can kill off the automatic things Amazon does to promote your book.

The worry a lot of folks have is that an image without a book cover on it may cause people to click thinking it's a show, movie, game, etc, and not buy once they realize the format. Too many of these will lower your conversion rate, and that will both cost money in junk clicks on the ad, and also train Amazon in a way you don't want.

They're not wrong. As such, putting a book cover on the ad—even if it increases the cost—is worth the higher conversion rate.

Math incoming!

Let's say you have an image with no book cover on it, and you're getting a cost per click of $0.10. Your conversion rate is 1 in 30, meaning it takes 30 clicks to make a sale.

CPR x Clicks to Make a Sale = Cost of Sale (CoS)

$0.10 x 30 = $3.00

Now, let's say that with a book cover on the ad image, your CPC climbs to $0.15, but your conversion rate improves to 1 in 20.

CoS: $0.15 x 20 = $3.00

With that change, it's a wash, but what if the conversion rate improves just a little more, to 1 in 15?

CoS: $0.15 x 15 = $2.25

Now we're cooking! That's $0.75 more earned per sale, and on a $3.99 title (which pays $2.70 in royalties), the ad is now profitable on the first book sold, without relying on read-through to make a positive ROI.

Not only that, but it trains Amazon in a positive manner.

MY COUNTER-COUNTERARGUMENT

What if there's a *best of both worlds* situation?

The answer to that question is back a few pages, where I talked about different types of headlines. By using a headline that has words like "read," "book," "author," "novel," etc, we can plant the knowledge that the ad is for a book in someone's subconsciousness without them even reading the ad in great detail.

Then, provided they at least skimmed over the text, we can reduce the number of people who click thinking the ad is for a show, movie, etc...

Of course, there's no golden rule, and your combination of genre, images, book, ad copy, audience, and targeting is different than anyone else's. That means the only way to know for sure which will work best is to test different options.

We'll get into that in coming chapters, but now that you have some of the basic information at hand, let's talk about how to create/select the ideal images for your ad.

THE SCIENCE BEHIND IMAGES

You didn't think you could get through a text by me and *not* encounter a science lesson, did you?

Human eyes and perception have developed to pay extra attention to certain things, but first we have to *see* those things.

It's no secret that the higher the contrast, the better we can see. In a nutshell, white stands out against black better than a dark grey does.

Look for high contrast images. If you're not sure if an image is high contrast, put it in some editing software and flip it to black and white.

Below is an example of a lower-contrast image.

And now in black and white.

You can see that, barring a few areas, this image is mostly grey on grey. However, with just about any half-decent image editing software, we can crank up the contrast, and then the brightness, to get this result:

And back in color, with some added saturation in the mix:

Compare the two images. Which do you think would grab your attention more as you're scrolling through your Facebook feed?

NEGATIVE SPACE AND CROPPING

The image below has a lot of negative space around the tree. What this does is draw the eye directly to the focal point of the image. The open space around the tree makes for a sense of wonder and grandeur.

The (current) ideal aspect ratio on social media ads is a square. This is how I would crop this tree down to a square:

I'm keeping the tree off-center to keep a little of the wide-image feeling. Even with the focus a lot tighter on the tree, we still get that "lone tree on the hill" vibe.

However, if I center the tree and zoom in more, it becomes less about the setting and the sense of wonder it creates, and more about the tree itself.

That's perfect, if maybe your book cover has a really gnarly tree with some sort of special inscription on it that you want to highlight, but not if you want to show the broader setting.

The next set of crops highlights how moving the tree around can change the focus of the image and each could be used.

A) Is a bad crop (though the best of this batch). The tree is cut off in an odd spot. It's still the main focus of the image, but there's no room to add anything else (such as a 3D image of a book cover).

B) Here, we have a bit more room for a book cover. A bit more of the tree is cut off, which creates a feeling of curiosity about what's hidden, vs A, where it just looks like the tree didn't fit in the image properly.

C) Here, we have taken the tree and made it a background element. Now there is room for a book cover or some other element that can take the main focus.

D) In this crop, we have room for text or maybe a spread of books above the tree. The tree remains the primary focus, but there's room for secondary items.

CROPPING HUMANS

When done properly, cropping off parts of a person can add mystery and interest. Done wrong, it can look sloppy or like limbs have been amputated.

This is a basic diagram of where one should and should not crop. Obviously, there may be reasons to go against these guidelines for specific effects, but this is a good place to start.

I have a yellow marker right above the lips because that can be a tricky spot to crop, but, when done well, can be very powerful.

Cropping faces vertically has a few guidelines as well. The main idea is not to cut off ears, and not to slice too close to an eye (or through it). If you want to include both eyes, make sure that the crop line is as far from the eye as the distance from the eye to the center of the nose.

While these guidelines are useful for cropping any image one might use in their marketing, they're especially important when a cover is cropped.

Let's assume that I want to use the cover of my book *Outsystem*, but I don't have a version without the text in place. The percentage of the cover without text is fairly small, but there are still right and wrong ways to utilize it. In a), the image doesn't look good because the end of the gun is missing and it creates an odd feeling of incompleteness. In b), that's corrected, and we've cropped Tanis at an acceptable point, but now there's so much negative space that she's not the focus of the image. That's solved in c) by putting in a 3D book cover!

Next up, d) is an example of a rather excessive crop of the character that focuses the image on the gun, not her. The e) iteration doesn't solve that issue, though it does make the character look more central to the image. However, f) is the ideal way to crop this image, if we wish to keep Tanis as the primary focus and not add in another element.

GENRE AND TROPES

Ads are the ideal way to capture readers who may not be pulled in by your cover art. This is where stock photos come into play.

Authors often get hung up on art that accurately depicts a scene from their book. That can be very difficult to find on stock photo sites, and may be rather limiting.

A stock photo used for an ad needs to do three things.

1. Not misrepresent the book in a significant way. For example, one shouldn't use a picture of a horse if there are no horses in the book.
2. Clearly convey the genre the book is in.
3. Clearly convey 2+ major tropes in the book.

This image clearly has a dystopian or urban fantasy vibe. It also carries the strong young woman trope, and her expression and outfit also convey a dark element.

In the next image, it probably goes without saying that the book is steampunk. On top of that, we have a strong female trope, as well as a bit of a badass bitch trope.

While the woman in the first image was mysterious and broody, the woman in the second looks more likely to punch someone in the face than hem and haw over how to defeat the dark lord without losing her soul.

On the opposite page are a few images I've used in ads recently. Some were adjusted for contrast, and some were combined with other elements, but these are all pictures I got off stock photo websites with just a few minutes of searching.

PART 3: ADVERTISING CAMPAIGNS

Gah! "Advertising Campaigns". Doesn't that just sound awful? It's so formal and marketing-y.

I should say that I happen to like marketing—especially when I believe in the product. So I hope you understand that I'm not bashing marketers, honest.

Nevertheless, the term just feels so dry!

NOTE: Make sure you set up a Facebook business account before proceeding. This way, if your account gets blocked for some reason (such as an ad that violates the rules), it is (usually) just the business part that is restricted, not your personal account.

Likewise, if your personal account runs into trouble, your business account can still be accessed (though you need to grant another trusted person access to the account).

Visit https://business.facebook.com to create your account.

Let's get into what a marketing campaign in Facebook is, and what it means to you.

A "campaign" typically encompasses all your efforts to move a particular product down a particular funnel.

In our case, that's usually the first book in a series, and the funnel is three steps:

1. See ad and click
2. Land on Amazon page (or page of other retailer)
3. Buy

Or, if you're advertising for leads, your funnel is five steps:

1. See ad and click
2. Land on offer (like a Book Funnel page for your book, or a signup form you manage) and submit.
3. Get marketing email and click
4. Land on Amazon page (or page of other retailer)
5. Buy

Typically, the shorter the funnel, the better it converts.

Some products (like cars, televisions, computers, expensive enterprise business products) have long funnels because the seller has a lot of explaining, and convincing, to do.

However, when it comes to books, the main thing we're convincing people to do is spend a few hours reading our story. Our tools for doing that are the cover, title, blurb, and price. Thise can all be found on the retailer's product display page, so get the reader to that page without delay.

And now, as quickly as I can manage, here's the breakdown of the campaign types and how they apply to your business.

CAMPAIGN TYPES

When you go into Facebook's Ad Manager interface and click that "Create Ad" button, you're faced with six types of campaigns you can build.

The first option is **"Awareness"**. These types of ads are for getting likes on a page, or making people aware of your brand. They are aimed more at products sold in brick-and-mortar stores; things like laundry detergent or a six-pack of cola work well here. Users of these advertisements just want to remind people that "Tide Rocks!", so the next time a person is out picking up some detergent, that's the brand they buy.

These awareness ads are not terribly effective for us, but they can be used to build up fan pages, which I'll get into later.

Next up is **"Traffic"**, which is the type authors use most. What we want to do is drive traffic to our Amazon (or other retailer) product page.

That page (if you have a good blurb, cover, price, and Look Inside) should already be a fine-tuned selling machine. If it's not, your conversion rate of ad clicks to sales (once this is all done) will tell you.

The fewer steps there are between the user and that page, the better.

> **Now, I hear you all the way over here.** *"I've got this sweet landing page I've made on my website, and it is a thing of beauty!"*

I don't doubt you, but no matter how good you are at making a landing page, Amazon's product page has decades of *science* behind it. It's built to sell. Not only that, but it's familiar to your visitors, and probably more trusted. They like that page. It's where they buy everything, from car parts, to shoes, to groceries. Leverage that.

Also, you have three clicks before users start to get all "meh" about buying anything on the internet. Your ad and the Buy button on Amazon are two of those clicks. If they had to open the book, or dig into reviews, you've used up another one or two. Do you really want to insert *your* page on *your* site in the middle of that?

However, don't take my word for it. When you create your ad later, do an A/B test, with one ad going to your page first, and another going right to Amazon. Put different tracking codes on each, and see which way works better.

I'll be right most of the time, but I may be wrong in your case, and I am fully prepared to celebrate your success with you.

The **Engagement** types are ads geared toward starting conversations with people. **Leads** are ads with a goal of getting a user to fill out a lead capture form on Facebook. **App Promotion** is just what it sounds like, and **Sales** are ads set up to sell a product directly on Facebook using their product catalog system.

TRAFFIC ADS

Select "Traffic" and scroll down. You'll get the option to name the campaign, Ad Set, and individual ad. I generally do this right away, so I don't end up with a bunch of ads labeled "New Traffic Ad".

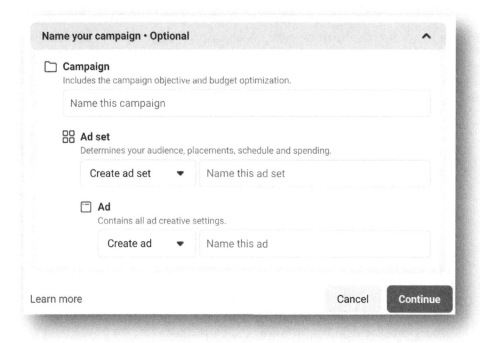

Once you've done that, click "Continue". On the next page, you'll be presented with a few options you can tweak. For ninety-nine percent of ads that authors run, we don't need to change anything, so click "Next" and we'll move on.

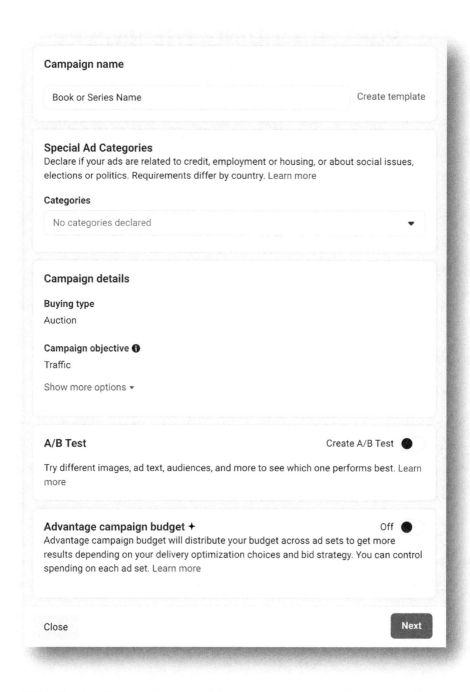

OK! On to the Ad Set, which is where we pick who will see our ad.

PART 4: FINDING THE RIGHT AUDIENCE

If you've been at this book-marketing game for a while—or have been writing to market—then this is not a new topic for you.

Audience is something we as writers think about a lot. Who wants to read our books? Why? What else do they like to read?

What we'll cover here is how to create Facebook's version of an audience, using some of the same tips and tricks you already know, and maybe a few new ones.

Of all the steps in making a good ad, this is the one with the most data, yet it is still a black box. You can easily find groups of people interested in other authors you *think* are similar to you, but you really have no idea if they'll respond to your ads and ultimately buy or borrow your book.

Though we sometimes think of our readers this way, at its heart, your audience is not defined by categories, metrics, or anything other than the type of escapism they prefer to engage in.

If you can figure out what sort of books your audience likes to read, you're in business. If you've written books that *you* like to read, then this part is a breeze: it's probably the contents of your own bookshelf.

SETTING UP THE AUDIENCE IN FACEBOOK'S AD MANAGER

As discussed in the previous section, a campaign is a bucket of "Ad Sets" that are trying to drive a particular type of activity. In our case, this is "Traffic".

If you skipped the chapter above, and are about to click anything other than "Traffic" when creating your campaign, please go back and read the descriptions to be certain you understand the implications of your decision.

Before we get to setting up our Audience, we have to make our campaign. Here are the quick steps, once more:

1. Go to the Facebook Ad Manager
2. Click "Create Ad"
3. Pick "Traffic" from the list of campaign types
4. Enter a name other than "Traffic" in the box that appears below (usually your book title)
5. Click "Continue"

THE AD SET

The "Ad Set" is a smaller bucket within the Campaign that contains elements shared by all ads beneath it.

There are a lot of options on this page, but not all are ones we'll make use of. I'll walk through the options section by section.

Note: Facebook likes to test out changes on small groups of users, so your page may not be in the same order as this.

1. Conversion
2. Dynamic Creative
3. Budget & Schedule
4. Audience
5. Placements
6. Optimization & Delivery

CONVERSION

Conversion is almost always set to website by default, but sometimes Facebook gets tricksy, so be sure it's set to website (which will be the retailer product page).

Conversion

Conversion location
Choose where you want to drive traffic. You'll enter more details about the destination later.

● Website
Send traffic to your website.

DYNAMIC CREATIVE

We talked about Dynamic Creative in the prior chapter, and I *highly* recommend using it. It has to be turned on in the Ad Set before the ad is published, so do that now.

Dynamic creative On
Provide creative elements, such as images and headlines, and we'll automatically generate combinations optimized for your audience. Variations may include different formats, templates or audio based on one or more elements. Learn more

The following message will appear, outlining some of the changes. None of those will hamper our efforts, so click "Continue" and away we'll go.

How to create ads using dynamic creative ✕

You can now provide creative elements, such as images and headlines, that will be used to automatically generate variations for your audience.

Certain variations, such as automatically cropping an image or applying a carousel template, depend on the creative elements and placements selected.

Some settings, such as send to Messenger, are not yet available for ads using dynamic creative. Those settings will be disabled.

Cancel   Continue

BUDGET & SCHEDULE

A good daily budget to start with is $5. The reason for a low starting budget is that you don't know if the ad is any good yet, and neither does Facebook. Until you start to prove out that ad, you want to keep your spending low. I get into scaling good ads a lot more in the "Tuning Ads" section.

Leave all the other settings on their defaults. Later, we'll discuss end dates, lifetime budgets, and ad scheduling.

OPTIMIZATION AND DELIVERY

Depending on which version of the Ad Manager you see, this could look one of two ways.

The next screenshot shows the old way, which has been standard for a few years. Some people—mostly in the UK, at present—don't have an "Optimization & Delivery" section. Instead, those options are merged into the "Conversion" section at the top of the page.

Some of the labels are a little different in these two sections, but they ultimately do the same thing.

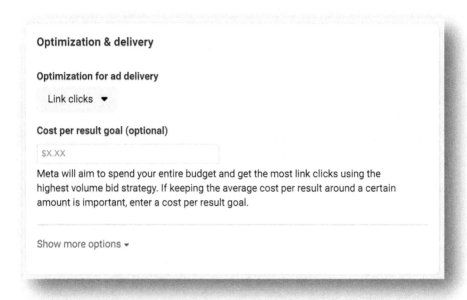

Below is the new version that will become more common.

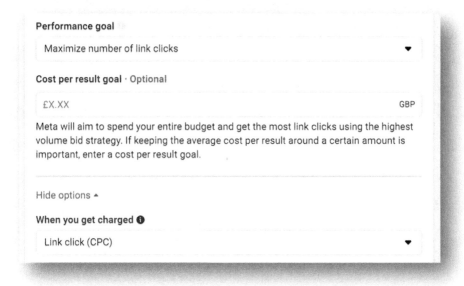

On the old setup, "Optimization for ad delivery" is set to "Link Clicks", and we do not want to change it. On the new version, this is called "Performance goal" and is often set to "Maximize number of landing page views" by default.

If yours is set to this, change it to "Maximize number of link clicks".

Next up is the "Cost per result goal". This is where you can set a sort of max CPC. Don't fill this in; contrary to expectations, it tends to drive up the CPC.

Finally, at the bottom of both versions is a text link that says "Show more options". Click to expand it and then open up the "When you get charged" dropdown. If you have the option to choose "Link click (CPC)", do so. If it's greyed out, it should become an option after your account is older.

Flipping this option probably doesn't change too much behind the scenes, but from testing I've done, it seems to show the ad more to people who are likely to click.

THE AUDIENCE

Whew! It sure took a bit to get here, but I hope you learned something along the way. This is where we really get into the nuts and bolts of building an actual ad; thus, where the fun starts!

Audience

Define who you want to see your ads. Learn more

New audience ▼

Custom audiences   Create new ▼

Reach people who interacted with your business or others who may be similar.

🔍 Search existing audiences

Exclude

* Locations

• United States

Age

18 ▼   65+ ▼

Selecting an audience under 18 will limit your targeting options to some locations and age. Learn more

Gender

⦿ All   Men   Women

Detailed targeting

Include people who match ❶

🔍 Add demographics, interests or behaviors   Suggestions **Browse**

Exclude

Advantage detailed targeting ✦
    Reach people beyond your detailed targeting selections when it's likely to improve
    performance.

Languages

All languages

Note: there is an older version of this section that looks slightly different, but the elements are the same, they just have a different visual appearance.

OK, so now that we're in the audience section, all you have to type in is: "all the people who will love my book".

Jackpot! Print money.

No?

Sadly, there is no magic bullet here, and this little box is the most powerful, and most nuanced part of Facebook advertising. You can build an audience six ways from Sunday; however, you can do it wrong more easily than you can do it right.

Let's start from the top.

CUSTOM AUDIENCES

These types of audiences are built on people's activity as it pertains to you and your properties.

By properties, I mean things such as:

- Facebook page
- Instagram account
- Email address list
- Website activity
- Interaction on videos

Provided these properties are connected to your Facebook account (more on that later), you can target anyone who has interacted with your content in these places and show them ads.

This is most useful in retargeting ads.

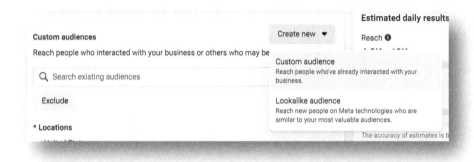

To create a new custom audience, click the "Create New" button and then choose "Custom Audience". "Lookalike" audiences are built on custom audiences you've already made, so we have to start there first.

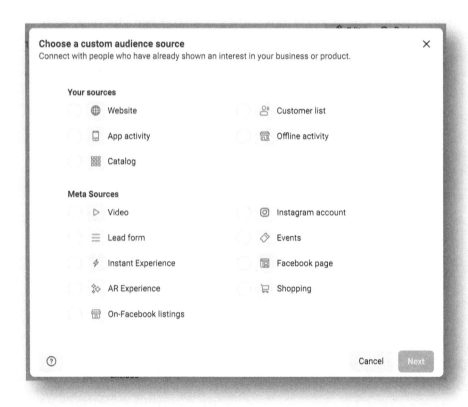

This is the full list of sources that can be used to create a custom audience. Getting into the nitty gritty of these audiences is beyond the scope of this book—it's nearly a full book on its own, but we do offer video classes on how to leverage this element.

There are also examples further on in this book.

LOOKALIKE AUDIENCE

A lookalike audience takes a custom audience you already have (say, everyone who likes your Facebook page) and finds other people like them.

Some folks use this with success, but it's not for the reasons they may think.

If we take a moment to consider who Facebook's main users are for its ads platform, it doesn't take long to realize it's not authors. We're probably the only people on Earth using the platform to sell a $4 product.

The advertisers they really care about sell bigger ticket items, such as washing machines, phones, cars, vacations, etc....

Once we knew Facebook does this, the answer to how lookalike audiences are built becomes clear.

They're based on demographics and buying power. Factors like education level, income bracket, age, gender, whether a person has children/grandchildren, whether they own their own home or rent, whether they own their car or lease....

The list goes on. Somewhere, probably down at the bottom, is whether they read.

But realistically, when the Facebook data AIs go off to find folks like those who follow your page, chances are those results are based on how much money they make, their age, and where they live.

Granted, in a number of genres, that probably works out alright. In the case of romance, it's not a problem at all. Given that 50% of women in the USA read romance, any random sampling of women is going to have the same percentage of romance readers as any other sampling.

Now, a lookalike audience with a sufficiently large sample—something over fifty thousand people—can work relatively well, so if you have that sort of activity on your properties, then you could make this work.

The caveat with lookalike audiences is that they are, at most, 10% of a country's population—and generally work best if kept under 3%.

However, if you consider that (in the USA) there are about 10 million readers in most major genres, a 3% lookalike audience (which comes to 8.1 million people) is smaller than the total audience available.

Now, you may be thinking that 8.1 million people is still *a lot*, and you'd be right! But we don't know for sure that all of those people read a given genre, or that they're even readers at all.

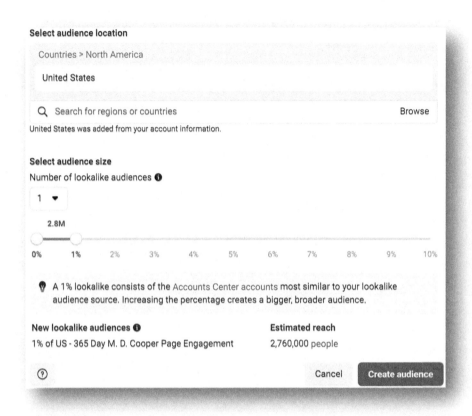

Now, you may be thinking that 8.1 million people is still *a lot*, and you'd be right! But we don't know for sure that all of those people read a given genre, or that they're even readers at all.

That means we still have to narrow down the audience. Most of the time, we end up with only twenty to thirty percent of the total lookalike size.

Because of this, I generally don't use them. I feel I can do better with direct targeting. But your mileage may vary.

LOCATION, AGE, & GENDER

This section is pretty straightforward, but very important to get right. There are pitfalls that can eat up *all* your money and give you nothing in return.

First up is the Country.

Let's be frank; to start with, focus on the USA and UK. Other countries don't matter that much (sorry, Canada and Australia) because their populations are so small.

Focusing on Canada and Australia is like spending special effort to market to Florida...Well, except that more people live in Florida.

I'm Canadian, and I accept this; I know you'll be able to, as well.

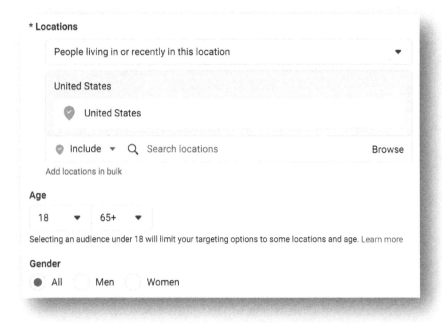

EXCEPTION NOTICES

There are always exceptions, right? This is no different. There are times when it makes a lot of sense to advertise to Canada and Australia.

One is when you have an ad that was once working well, but now isn't doing much in the UK or USA anymore. You can just swap it over to one of those countries for a bit!

The other exception is if you're wide.

Kobo has a huge presence in Canada, so I often run Kobo ads aimed at the Canadian market. And Australia has a very strong iBook market, so ads aimed there for that purpose can be very effective.

Another scenario is if you have some sort of hyper-regional target for your book, like a story that takes place on the campus of a well-known university. In that case, you'll want to make sure you pick the right place—although, you may find that Facebook ads aren't profitable for that.

I used to also target Germany, but the KU page-read rate is a lot lower there, so I don't bother (it's fine for German language books, because their words are so freaking long, but English books in Germany suffer because of that low page-reads rate).

Also, make a separate ad for the USA and the UK. For now, pick both those countries; when you start getting clicks on your ad, you'll see why you may want to break them apart. We'll get into separating them in a later section.

> Whatever you do, *DO NOT* pick India, Philippines, or other countries in South-East Asia. Folks in these countries are low competition, so clicks are cheap. Facebook will optimize for that and spend your budget on audiences that don't convert to sales.

Next up, pick your age group. I never bother with people under the age of 24—they're broke, and/or don't seem to read. Kidding; they don't seem to read *my* stuff. If you're targeting them, you should, of course, pick them.

Again, we'll get into reading the stats later, and you can see which age groups are most cost effective for you to market to. For my books, I start my target age range at 35-65+ as a safe bet, and sometimes prune further once I get solid stats.

WARNING: MINDSET SHIFT AHEAD

Remember, your marketing targets may not completely align with your main reader demographic. Hypothetically, you could have a huge readership (60% of your readers, for instance) below the age of 20. But folks that age are not frequent Facebook users, so you'll have to target them elsewhere.

However, in this scenario, 40% of your demographic is over 20, *and* are on Facebook. Well, well! Given population distribution (there are more older people on Earth), that's a bigger group of readers; potentially in the millions!

So remember, your ad is for a specific subset of your readers, defined by age, location, gender, and interests. A given ad's creative and audience target will not work for all your readers. Probably not even for 50% of your readers.

The last demographic to consider is gender (referring to Facebook's Male/Female gender selection for ad targeting). You can't be all things to everyone. You probably know whom you appeal to more, so pick that gender.

If you want to see how you perform with both genders, go for it, but keep an eye on the cost per result stats (again, these will be covered in the tuning section), as you'll find that your ad may cost a lot more with one gender than the other.

OK, THE *REALLY* FUN PART: SELECTING INTERESTS

Now we're at "Detailed Targeting". This is where we get to the meat (or soy... or cranberries; whatever your jam is) of the matter.

If you've selected keywords in an ad or online tool, this is basically your keywords section, but with a twist.

The twist is that Facebook only lets you pick things that have significant fan pages/interest groups on Facebook. The vast majority of indie authors aren't available to target, and even the lists of trad pub authors are short.

However, there are a number of ways to target readers. We'll go through three of them below.

TARGETING BY AUTHOR

The simplest, and most generally applicable way to target is by author name.

Chances are that you already know a few authors who write books like yours, so see if they're an option to target. If they're not, or you're not sure, check the bestseller lists on Amazon, or google "Best authors in _____ genre" and see if anyone online has handy lists for you.

As you add more authors, you'll see a count in the upper right of the screen showing how many people are in the audience you've selected. The goal is to reach a million, bare minimum. I wouldn't recommend going over ten million in most genres—except romance. There, I would keep it under twenty million.

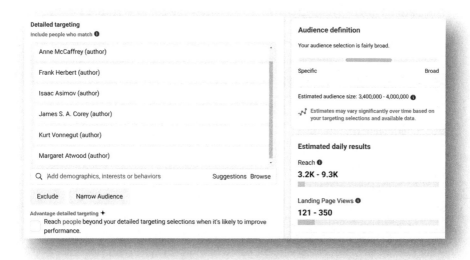

If you pick authors who don't have TV and movie deals, you don't need to do any further narrowing of the audience. If you end up selecting authors with content beyond the written medium, then click the "Narrow Audience" button and add in one of these interests depending on your genre/theme.

FICTION

Adventure Fiction

Cozy Mystery

Crime Fiction

Fantasy Books

Gothic Fiction

High Fantasy

Historical Mystery

Paranormal Romance

Romance Novels

Romantic Fantasy

Romantic Stories

Romantic Thriller

Spy Fiction

Supernatural Thrillers

Weird Fiction

Women's Fiction

Young Adult Fiction

Any other genres: Fiction Books, Literature, Novel, Short Story

NON-FICTION

There are fewer non-fiction options for narrowing audiences. Typically, I use "Non-Fiction Books" after selecting my main interest set.

All of these interests are literature/publications, which ensures that people with these interests are also readers. I no longer narrow by anything device-specific, such as: Amazon Kindle, eBook, and the like.

You can also group these together. For example, if you write thrillers with elements of suspense and mystery, you could narrow with both spy fiction and crime fiction.

Bonus: If you have audiobooks, add "Audiobooks" as one of the narrowing options. This isn't fiction/non-fiction specific, so you may pick up some folks who don't go for your type of book, but it can also get your ad in front of more of those sweet, sweet audiobook listeners.

TARGETING BY GENRE INTERESTS

As you saw above, there are a lot of general genre/theme interests. All of the ones I listed are specific to literature and publications. However, there are a number of more generic ones categorized as "entertainment & media".

In the next screenshot, you can see how each interest has parentheticals providing more information (thank you, Facebook people, for adding these. They are incredibly helpful).

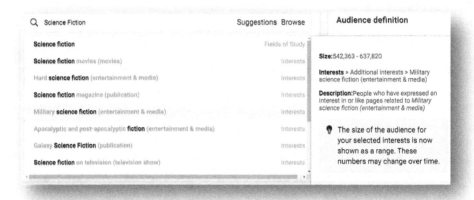

If you chose to build an audience using these types of interests and they are all literature/publications, then you don't need to narrow the audience.

However, if they include movies, television, or entertainment & media, then you'll need to narrow by the same interests (or any others relevant to literature/publication) as outlined at the end of the prior section.

WORD OF WARNING

A quick piece of advice is that if your cost-per-click is *super* high, then you are probably bidding for expensive keywords against a lot of other people. You may need to move down to a midlist author for your targeting, or remove any broad genre interests (like games, tv shows, or movies).

Conversely, if your cost-per-click is below $0.05, it may be that Facebook has targeted a group of users who are prone to click but not buy. Keep an eye on your conversions. If you aren't generating sales, remake the ad and audience to see if you can capture different readers.

LANGUAGES

I see a lot of folks select English US/English UK in the languages section, but Facebook advises against this (as do I). The reason being that the given options are for narrowing down to a minority language in a region, such as Spanish in the USA, or French in Canada.

It's best to leave that setting at its default.

ADVANTAGE DETAILED TARGETING

Advantage detailed targeting ✛
Reach people beyond your detailed targeting selections when it's likely to improve performance.

Leave this setting off. It is essentially layering a lookalike audience on top of the interests you've specified.

PLACEMENTS

Placements   Learn more

● Advantage+ placements (recommended) ✚
Use Advantage+ placements to maximize your budget and help show your ads to more people. Facebook's delivery system will allocate your ad set's budget across multiple placements based on where they're likely to perform best.

Manual placements
Manually choose the places to show your ad. The more placements you select, the more opportunities you'll have to reach your target audience and achieve your business goals.

Show more options ▾

At the bottom of the page lies the "Placements" section. This is how you control where the ad shows up on

Facebook/Instagram/etc.... Some folks recommend only displaying them on the Facebook feed, and there's nothing wrong with that. However, other placements can convert very well, and often have lower costs.

I recommend starting on the default setting, which is effectively "everywhere", and then removing placements that aren't performing after data has been gathered. We'll get into that in the section on tuning ads.

A FINAL TRICK

Let's be honest: guys can be...well, rude, in the comments they leave on ads, more so than women tend to be. It's often not intentional; men who frequently speak bluntly and without nonverbal cues to see how their tone is taken can come off as brusque.

However, they tend to curb that behavior when women are present. Yay for socialization! (I have no idea if I'm being sarcastic or not...)

This can work to your advantage. If you're advertising to men, pop into your reader group and ask the women to comment on an ad after you put it up. That helps your Social Proof, and will also cause men who come afterward to leave better comments. Hopefully.

SAVE YOUR AUDIENCE

Seriously. Save it. Whether it's good or bad, you want to remember these selections (especially if the audience doesn't work out—no need to target those folks again).

PART 5: CRAFTING THE AD

OK, I lied before; *this* is the fun part!

Once you've created, *and saved*, your Ad Set (which is where audience, placement, and daily budget all live), we get to the heart of things: the Ad itself.

IDENTITY

This is the first section, where you set the Facebook business page and Instagram account the ads will run under. These don't have to be connected to your Meta Business account (though it's ideal if they are), you just need to have access to the page and Instagram account.

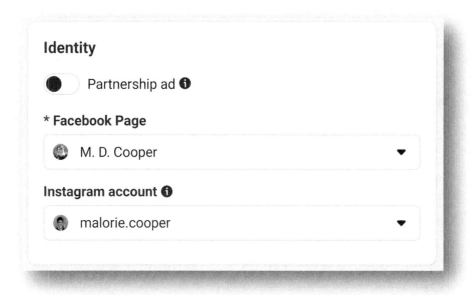

If you don't have an Instagram account, you'll have an option for the system to effectively make a fake one for you.

However, I recommend actually having an account on that platform to run your ads, even if you don't post often. It just lends a bit of extra cred.

Lastly, don't worry about the "Branded content ad" option, as those are for companies that are working with another to market a product.

AD SETUP

Though I *strenuously* recommend doing dynamic creative ads, I know that some folks like to leave less up to the AIs, and twiddle with the knobs themselves.

I'll walk through the options of both the standard "Ad setup", as well as the dynamic creative version.

DYNAMIC CREATIVE

In this type, we don't have the "Catalog" option. Catalogs are for when an advertiser sets up direct sales of the product through the Facebook platform. Authors do this very rarely, so it's no biggie that Dynamic Creative doesn't offer this.

Under the "Format" section, we have two options for how we want ads to show: a single image, or a carousel.

Carousel rarely works well for authors. It's geared more toward clothing companies, who may wish to show a lineup of fashions that a buyer can then scroll through and select any item.

Ad setup

Creative source

Choose how you'd like to provide the media for your ad.

- ● **Manual upload**
  Manually upload images or videos.

- ○ Catalog ✦
  Automatically use media from your catalog. We'll show each person the catalog items they're most likely to engage with.

Format

Dynamic creative is enabled. Multiple ads will be automatically generated using your individual creative assets.

- ● **Single image or video**
  One image or video, or a slideshow with multiple images

- ○ **Carousel**
  2 or more scrollable images

- ✓ **Multi-advertiser ads**
  Help people discover your products when they show commercial intent and are in a shopping mindset. Your ads may appear alongside ads from multiple businesses in Instagram feed. Learn more

Lastly, I leave "Multi-advertiser ads" turned on, as it can increase Instagram views and lower the cost on that platform, though probably not significantly.

Ad creative
Select the media, text and destination for your ad.

Website creative source
Find images from a page on your website to use in your ads.

| https://www.thewritingwives.com/event-de... | Approve |

By approving, you confirm that you have legal rights to use images found from the website provided for advertising.

* Media

| Select images | Select videos | Create Video |

Images, videos and slideshows   5 of 10

 🖼 1107 × 1107   ✕

Edit media

 🖼 1365 × 1365   ✕

Edit media

AD CREATIVE

This is the section where the remainder of the work is done in building the ad.

First up is image selection. With Dynamic Creative, we can put in up to ten images for Facebook to choose from. I generally start with four to seven, as it takes a while to get good data back on ten.

Both images and videos can be added to the media section. However, if you pick videos, make sure they're no more than twenty seconds long.

There are two ways to get the images up on Facebook. One is to put in a URL linking to a page on your website where you have them visible, the second is to upload them manually. The latter is what most people do.

Once you've loaded your images that we picked earlier, you'll want to crop them to be square*, if possible. Some just won't look good when cropped, so leaving those at their original proportions isn't the end of the world.

*Note: Some people don't have the option to crop to a square in the Ad Manager, so you may need to do that before uploading the images.

Every now and then, I test the 9:16 (vertical) orientation, because those ads are more likely to show with Stories and Reels, but the ratio seems to have higher CPCs.

Directly below the images is this toggle. Be certain to turn this *on*. It is crucial.

Optimize Creative For Each Person

Vary your ad creative and destination based on each person's likelihood to respond. See possible optimizations

What this does is create the ideal combination of text, image, and headline for a given person (as well as generates a handful of lesser optimizations).

This is where Dynamic Creative really shines. When this toggle is on, Facebook is using everything it has learned from a person's prior activities to determine what said person is most likely to engage with and click on.

With that toggle, we come to the end of the differences that Dynamic Creative brings. Let's look at the Standard creative setup now.

STANDARD CREATIVE

Standard Creative opens up the option to use a catalog of products being sold on Facebook for your chosen images, but since that rarely applies to authors (as we sell on retailers), we won't dig into it here.

The other option we get to display those images is Collection. Like Carousel, this is aimed more at people who sell products on Facebook, not folks like us who direct people to a retailer.

Ad setup

Create ad ▾

Creative source

Choose how you'd like to provide the media for your ad.

◉ Manual upload
Manually upload images or videos.

◯ Catalog ✦
Automatically use media from your catalog. We'll show each person the catalog items they're most likely to engage with.

Format

Choose how you'd like to structure your ad.

◉ Single image or video
One image or video, or a slideshow with multiple images

◯ Carousel
2 or more scrollable images or videos

◯ Collection
Group of items that opens into a fullscreen mobile experience

☑ Multi-advertiser ads
Help people discover your products when they show commercial intent and are in a shopping mindset. Your ads may appear alongside ads from multiple businesses in Instagram feed. Learn more

You may see an option in the "Ad Setup" section called "Standard Enhancements". This creates a number of slight alterations to your image that will make it stand out more and get more clicks.

If you see that option, it is beneficial to turn it on. If you do not, the option may appear on a subsequent screen which will be shown shortly.

My recommendation is to keep Multi-advertiser ads checked for the reasons listed in the Dynamic Creative section.

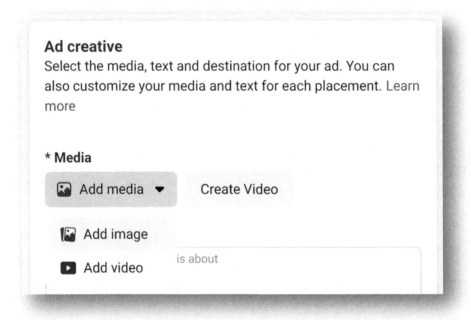

Next up is adding the image or video. Here, you have to pick one or the other. On the next page, you can choose from an image you've uploaded in the past, or upload a new one. Once an image is selected, the system will suggest ways to crop it for different placement types.

I recommend choosing crop options that remove the grey pillar-boxing and letterboxing.

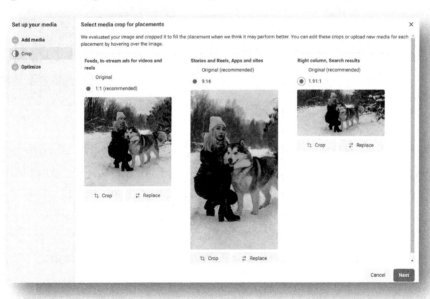

If the elements on the image aren't properly centered, click the "Crop" button and adjust them till they look good.

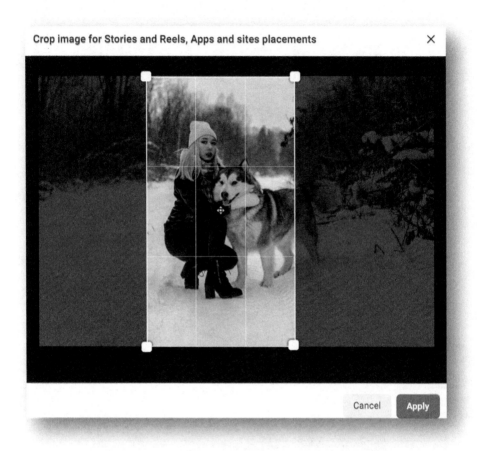

On the next screen, Facebook will present a number of image optimization options. Ideally, it's best to turn these on and let the AIs test things to find what works best.

If "Standard Enhancements" wasn't an option on a prior screen, this is where it will appear. Be sure to toggle it on.

There may also be a 3D animation option. I don't know that these work exceptionally well, but it may be worth testing.

Below are some examples of the automatic formatting that Facebook will create and test. It will typically prefer the ones that have the highest Result Rates and lowest CPRs.

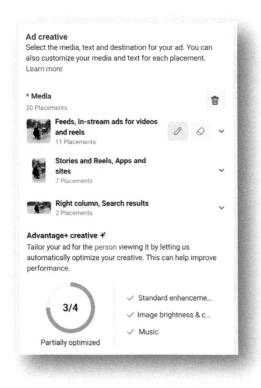

Other options are automated adjusting of brightness and contrast. This isn't necessary with high-quality images that already have good contrast, but if you're unsure about your image, turn it on.

Lastly is the option to automatically add music to your ad. I've not found this to have a material effect on ad performance one way or the other, so do what seems cool and fun to you.

With that complete, the image section will now look like the following screenshot.

PRIMARY TEXT AND HEADLINE

This section is pretty straightforward, especially if you've already created your ad copy. Whether you choose Dynamic Creative or not, you'll have the option to add multiple text options. To get the "Ad text option" button, you first have to click in the text field. Can add up to five variations.

Primary text

The Grange have returned, ghostly figures rising out of the snow beneath the pine boughs.

As the last remaining warden, Sarah must defeat them...or die trying.

Join Sarah on her journey into the fade.

eBook: https://amazon.com/dp/B008GZ8HEM
Print: https://amazon.com/dp/1477651527

One woman. One wolf. An army of the damned risen in the depths of winter.   ✕

eBook: https://amazon.com/dp/B008GZ8HEM
Print: https://amazon.com/dp/1477651527

⊕ Add text option

Headline · Optional

Lose yourself in the tale of one woman's war against the dead.

⊕ Add headline option

MULTIVARIATE TESTING

What we're doing here is something well beyond A/B Testing—we're doing Multivariate Testing, as we have more than two variables (A and B).

However, when testing a lot of variables at once, one can inadvertently create *a lot* of possible combinations.

To find out just how many, multiply the number of your image options (if you chose Dynamic Creative), Primary Text options, and Headline options.

For example, 5 images, 3 Primary Text sections, and 2 headlines comes to 30 ad combinations.

It's worth noting that Facebook does not create *all* possible combinations, just ones it thinks will work well. As it does that testing, it quickly prunes out those that do not get acceptable levels of engagement. Even so, try not to go above 30 combinations at once, as it can take a while to get good data on how they're all performing.

WHERE TO LINK YOUR AD (Website URL)

Remember the funnel. You want that funnel to be as short as possible, while still enticing the reader to buy. This means the fewer steps, the better.

Getting that reader right to the Amazon (or other retailer) product page, which is purpose-built to sell, is your number one goal. You should already have put significant effort behind a good cover, catchy blurb, and reader-grabbing peek inside; that being said, there are a few scenarios where you *might* want to send people to a page other than your Amazon product page.

1. You are advertising a multi-author promotion or giveaway. In this case, that URL is your destination page. It's where the "sale" happens.
2. You are running an ad for a reader magnet on a site like bookfunnel.com.
3. You are running a sale on multiple books and have created a landing page on your own site.

I did this recently, where I discounted three books in a series. To facilitate that, I ran single ads that landed the reader on a page that listed all three books with links to get them on sale.

A final question I know is burning a hole in your tongue is whether to send the reader to the product detail page for the first book in a series, or to the series page.

The answer is yes. Do both, and test to see which works better. Results vary book to book and audience to audience.

FURTHER AD COPY THOUGHTS & EXAMPLES

There are some additional ways to write ad copy. The first is to write it as "you," and the second is to write it as a marketer. The "you" version will be longer, and should bring out your passion about the story. The marketer version should be about the deal, ratings, reviews, awards, etc.

MARKETER'S VERSION

This one comes in two flavors. The first is what I call the "Pimpin'" ad. Here, you're flashing pedigree, reviews, a great price; you're pimpin' that puppy out.

PIMPIN' EXAMPLE

> BOOKNAME *by AUTHOR is rated as one of the best GENRE books out there. Top reviewer, NAME, said it lit his pants on fire! NYT best-selling AUTHOR is bringing his/her/their A-Game, and you don't want to miss out!*

The Pimpin' version is best suited for sales and deals, because it spotlights the quick facts and savings. "Get *BOOK* by AUTHOR this week only, for just 99c! Critics love it and rave...."

You get the picture.

I find that this type of blurb does not work for a long-running ad, and puts off a lot of readers (though it works for some).

CHALLENGE EXAMPLE

> *Is Malorie Cooper the next Isaac Asimov? Pick up a copy and find out for yourself!*

Well, that's pretty bold, isn't it? Some people may not be comfortable doing an ad like this, but they can really work. Just be prepared to police the ad's comments as the jerks show up.

That being said, Facebook doesn't really care much if comments are positive or negative. If people are engaging, the platform thinks your ad has value to their audience, and they show it more. *Any* comments are social proof.

Also, look at the stats for how many people have chosen not to have that ad, or any of your ads, shown to them again (which we'll get to in the tuning section), as you do want to make sure you're not putting people off too much.

YOUR VERSION

This one comes in several flavors. The first one is the "Flat-Out You" version.

FLAT-OUT YOU EXAMPLE

> *Hey, folks! I hope you don't mind me taking this little bit of your Facebook news feed, but I wanted to tell you about my latest book that is fan-freaking-tastic. It has dragons, an evil wizard, and a young lad who has to beat all the odds. I wrote it in an LSD-fueled haze, and it was amazeballs (the LSD and the book). You're gonna love it.*

This type of copy works best when you're making ads for people who have liked your page or who really have a close set of interests related to your book.

These people already know you and your voice, and will respond well to this use of it. Also, they are often just in need of a small reminder that your next book is out and waiting for them to devour.

These ads have the benefit of being genuine, which a lot of people really like and engage with.

PLOT-BASED EXAMPLE

> *Dragons rule the land, and no one is safe. Even those who do attempt to venture out of their holds in defiance of the beasts find themselves attacked by the evil wizard. Only one young man possesses the power to defeat all the bad guys and save the day!*

This is the type of ad that people always tell you *not* to make. They tell you to make the marketer's ad. But for most authors, that's just not who we are; we're storytellers. That's our jam.

I say we should embrace that.

Our readers come to us for stories. What better way to get that story across to them than in the ad? Tell them about the grand adventure that awaits them, a tale of swordplay, or love, or desperate times!

You (should) have a strong emotional attachment to your book and know why you love it. This is a strength. Use it.

When you're done writing this ad, read it aloud in a movie announcer voice. If it doesn't make you want to rush to the theater to see it on the big screen, keep working till it does.

CHARACTER-BASED BLURB

> Jimmy has lived all his life in Grimlock Hold, scraping by to get food and shelter, and survive the daily rain of dragon poop. But one day, through some amazing circumstance, Jimmy discovers that he has a stupendous destiny to save the world (plus the girl— if she doesn't save him first)!

The character-based blurb is really just a twist on the plot-based one. There's a reason for this: some people prefer character-driven stories, while other people prefer plot-driven stories.

Chances are that your story is both. So make an ad for each element and run both. What you'll find about ¾ of the time is that your plot-driven ads will resonate better with men, and character-based ads will resonate better with women.

That's not to say that women don't like plots, and men don't like characters. It's just that gender is a useful indicator as to a *preference* for one over the other.

However, experimentation is key. Disparate demographics, markets, and genres will yield different results.

I had an ad that I was *certain* would not appeal to women, and so, for five months, I only targeted men. Then, as I began to saturate that audience, I decided to duplicate the Ad Set (since that's where the audience is contained), add one reference to the main character in the story, and put that ad in front of women.

And it did great! It cost about $0.10 more per click than it did for men, but it was still within my tolerance for a positive ROI, and I reached a brand-new audience with the ad.

THE FUN AD EXAMPLE

Who doesn't like to have a bit of fun?

> *Right after Jimmy finishes his after-school snack, he's gotta go save the world—or at least his town. That is, if his mom doesn't make him clean his room first.*
>
> *He'd better get to it, or plant-eating zombies are gonna be everywhere!*

Ads like this pair well with funny and food-related images. People engage with them more, and the more engagement your ad gets, the less Facebook charges you for your clicks.

Obviously, you can't do this style for a tragic book. But if your story has humorous elements, you can certainly pick out a few and make a fun ad that shows off that tone.

YOUR AD IS COMPLETE!

OK, it's not actually complete. First, you need to pick your call to action button. I really wish there was one that simply said, "BUY!" but there isn't. So I vacillate between "Download" and "Learn More".

The effectiveness of one button text over the other probably has more to do with the ad copy than anything else. Feel free to experiment.

But before you publish the ad, here's one last thing to consider:

SHAMELESS SELF-PROMOTION

No, not for me; for you. That's what ads are...you are promoting yourself. And that can feel damn awkward. On the flipside, folks who do a lot of marketing tend to forget that it is *supposed* to be damn awkward.

The more you advertise and promote, the more you start to think of yourself and your books as a brand. You detach yourself from it all and treat it like not-you. That is OK. It's natural, and I'm sure there's even some name for it.

But be careful. Your readers don't see you that way.

They see self-promotion as a bit distasteful, and they like authors because they feel like they're making a connection with a human telling them a story.

You need to keep this in mind as you make your ads.

Self-promotion works best if it's coming from the "raw you" talking directly to the reader, or if it's highlighting a deal. They don't care if you're shamelessly pimping yourself if they get a bargain in the mix! ;)

PAY NO ATTENTION TO THE MAN BEHIND THE CURTAIN!

There is a way to have the best of both worlds, and it is to not run your ads as you. People will respond to a recommendation from a 3rd party far better than they will to one from you directly. This is obvious; this is why we do NL swaps, and use paid book services. It's why reviews matter, and why social proof is huge.

So how do you do it for your FB ads?

Here's the deal. You have your author page, where you talk to folks, push your deals and wares, and post snippets and cover reveals. This is you. Run your "raw you" ads from this page. Don't run your market-y/plot/character ads from this page, because they aren't coming from "you".

What you need to do (and this will take time—a *good bit* of time) is make a new genre fan page. If it's SF, you could make it about a trope, or maybe about some good books or TV series. If it's UF, you could make a Buffy fan page, or a general genre page like "Great Romance books I Love".

Run your ads as that page. Pimp other people's books there (good books that you believe in), and you'll build trust with folks who like and follow the page. That way, when you promote *your* book on this page, people will trust you and they'll check it out.

Keep in mind, though, you need to run that page as a faceless marketer. It only works if you create a marketing persona for yourself, and run the genre/fan page as them. Some people can't do that. If that's the case, work out a way where you can run it more as "you," but be prepared to lose some of the advantage of the "trusted recommender" promoting your books.

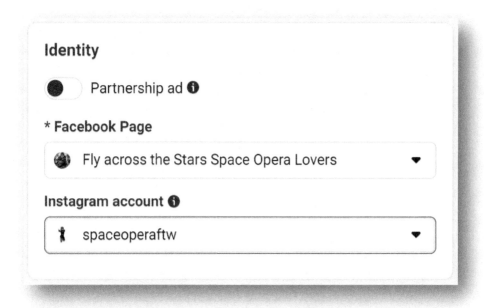

Do not pay for likes, or run giveaways to build followers on this page. You want this page to be for true lovers of what you're putting up there. As you run ads from this platform, you will get people liking the page. I know; crazy, right? People will click "like" on the sponsor of an ad!

It does take a year or so to build up a genre-based fan page organically (at least, it did for me). But when it's built, it will be just as powerful as a newsletter, and will give you an additional avenue for marketing and promotion.

PUBLISH THAT AD!

OK, we're ready to submit the ad, so go forth and do it.

Some things to remember (and to double-check, which you can do by clicking along the list of steps on the left side of the page):

1. Budget should be set to $5
2. Pick a country
3. Narrow to one gender
4. Write copy like you're a human, not a marketing robot
5. High contrast images that convey the genre and major tropes in your book
6. Remember what *you* love about your work, and sell the emotion

Your ad will take a bit of time to get approved (though it's faster when there's no text in the image), and then once it has, the stats can have a few hours' delay.

What we're doing at this point is seeing how the ad resonates with your market. If you have a killer ad, you'll know this in one day. You may also have a fantastic ad that will take 2 days to prove out. Expect to spend $10-$15 for each ad you test. If you're on day three and the ad isn't picking up steam, then it's time to axe it.

"So, how do I really know if my ad is working?"

Read on, gentle reader, read on...

PART 6: ANALYZING ADS

Before I get into examining your ad's performance, I want to talk about failure.

I used to work as a software architect, and the one thing we worked hard at was detecting failure—and doing so as quickly as possible. We weren't just looking for errors in programming, but also in our thinking. A slogan we adopted was "fail fast".

The same thing is true in ads. You aren't going to make a perfect ad the first time around. Or the second, or the third. Just like your writing, this is a craft that you must hone and continuously improve.

Also, most of us writers are great at long-form writing, and terrible at short-form. It's just not something we do that often. That's why I'm a believer in the story ad; an ad that highlights your story and your storytelling abilities.

What "fail fast" means for us, is that you need to constantly look for ads (and individual creative elements) that *aren't* working, as much as you need to identify the ones that are performing well.

Also, *every* ad will eventually stop working, so failure is a state that every ad will reach at some point.

SPENDING MONEY

The other thing you need to think about is how much capital you can invest in ads before you see a return.

Let's look at a moderately successful scenario:

You're running ads at $5/day, and your first three flop. Each of those flops took three days to prove out as failures. That means you've spent $45 on failure. This is okay! Note what didn't work, and don't do that again.

You did so, and now ad #4 is ticking along and getting you clicks at a good CPC. Sales are starting to roll in.

Keep in mind that sales can lag by days in some cases, so you may see clicks for a few days and not many sales, but two to three days later, those sales will appear.

If you're in KU, it will take longer. This is because someone borrowing your book may not immediately read it. The time from the initial borrow to a complete-read of a KU book can be as long as six weeks.

Alright, because you're not made of money, you keep ad #4 running at $5/day for two months. That's how long you'll have to wait, give or take a bit, before Amazon pays you for those sales that you made when your ad started to roll.

At this point, you've fronted $345 on ads. Can you tolerate that sort of spending until you get a return?

Be aware of this cashflow delay, and plan for it.

You can also pause an ad and start it back up later. You don't lose your social proof, though FB may temporarily charge you more per click when it's restarted.

OK, so failure costs you $45, and success costs you another $300. That's a good baseline to start with. Be ready to spend that money before you begin.

THE THREE MOST IMPORTANT METRICS

Over the past three years, I've worked with hundreds of authors, creating and honing ads in nearly every genre of fiction, and many categories of non-fiction.

That broad experience has given me the opportunity to really dig into the numbers and sort out what data indicates how the ad is working. I've spent months tracking every variable across a hundred ads, endeavoring to sort out which datapoints would tell me if an ad was healthy or not.

At the end of that process, I narrowed it down to three.

- Cost per Result
- Result Rate
- Frequency

By looking at just these, I can assess an ad's health and make decisions about it. Now, I often dig deeper and (of course) look at trends, but these are my bellwethers.

THE OTHER METRICS I'VE USED

Back in the days of this book's first edition, the number to use was "Relevancy". This was a good barometer for knowing if your ad was hitting its mark with users, and I really liked it for its simplicity.

However, around 2020, Facebook retired this metric. Before doing so, they introduced three new ones as its replacement: Quality, Engagement Rate, Conversion Rate.

These three new ratings are still available and will display the following data:

- Above Average
- Average
- Below average (Bottom 35% of ads)
- Below average (Bottom 20% of ads)
- Below average (Bottom 10% of ads)

Not to put too fine a point on it, but this data sucks. We don't really know what percentages define "Average" and "Above Average", which means we just know that we want one of those two classifications.

On top of that, these values don't populate for Dynamic Creative ads. Which is unfortunate, since those are the types I recommend most.

However, there is another metric that is available in every situation and tells us everything we need to know.

INTRODUCING: RESULT RATE

This is where the angelic chorus sings. Honest.

Result rate is the percentage of people who see your ad, and then carry out the action (this is the result). For a traffic ad, that result is clicking the link.

This parameter is not on by default, so we'll need to enable it. While we're at it, we'll enable Frequency as well, since it's one of the other three metrics that are key to analyzing an ad.

To enable these, click the "Columns" link in the upper right of the Ad Manager.

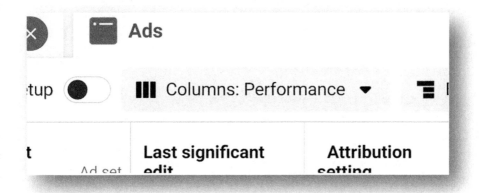

From the dropdown that appears, choose "Customize Columns". This will load a screen where you can alter the columns that show on your Ad Manager.

Check off "Result rate" and "Frequency". They're right near the top. Once they're added, they'll go to the bottom of the list of columns on the right side of the page. Drag them up so that they're right below "Cost per result".

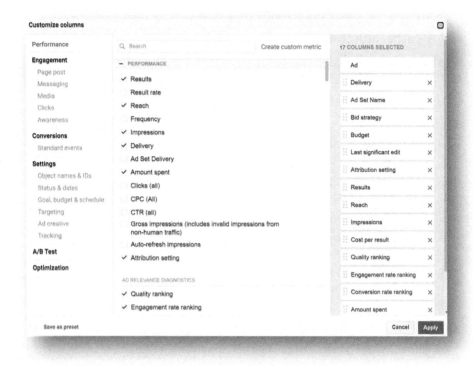

Then click the "Apply" button. This will prompt the new columns to appear. Lastly, save these columns and set them as your default. To do so, click the "Columns" button again and click the "Save" link beside the custom selection.

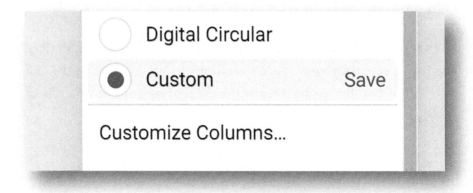

Next, enter a name.

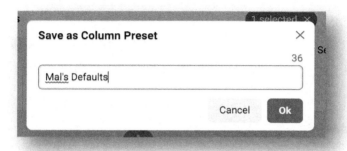

Then make that preset the default (if you wish) by clicking "Set as Default".

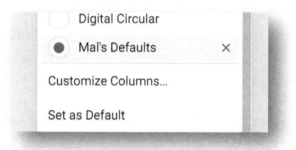

This is what the new columns will look like:

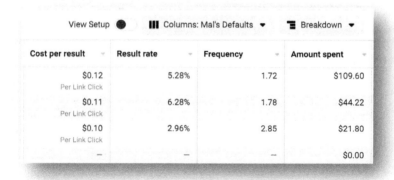

UNDERSTANDING THE RESULT RATE

The thing I love about the result rate is that it is essentially the same thing as the old relevancy score, but much more granular. As I said above, it is the percentage of people who see your ad and generate a result (click the link).

The higher this percentage, the more the ad is resonating with its audience.

Result Rate is not a one-size-fits-all measurement. For example, it's relatively easy to get a contemporary romance novel ad's result rate up over 10%. It's even possible to get them as high as 20%.

However, for more niche genres, such as Military Science Fiction featuring queer female lead characters (what I write), 4% is a sufficient rate.

Here is a breakdown of what I consider acceptable for well-performing ads in a variety of genres. The lower number is where I'd examine the ad to see if it needs to be re-worked, while the upper is an excellent ad.

- Contemporary Romance: 8% - 20%
- Small Town/Clean Romance: 6% - 15%
- MM Romance: 6% - 15%
- Genre Romance (Paranormal, RH, etc...): 5% - 10%
- Thrillers/Suspense/Mainstream Mystery: 8% - 16%
- Cozy/Niche Mystery: 5% - 10%
- Urban Fantasy/Paranormal/PWF: 4% - 9%
- Mainstream Science Fiction/Fantasy: 4% - 8%
- Niche Science Fiction/Fantasy/Genre: 2% - 6%

I didn't list every genre, because that would take some time, but the basic tenet is that for mainstream romance, the result rate should be over 10%, and for most everything else, the floor is 4% – 6%.

One thing to consider, however, is that insofar as audience appeal and conversion is concerned, your ads are not competing against other *people,* so much as one another.

What I mean by this is if you have two ads for the same book (targeting different audiences), and both have acceptable Cost Per Result numbers, but one has a 3% result rate and the other has a 9% Result Rate, you have a pretty good idea which one you'll want to improve, and which to possibly turn off.

To summarize, an ad's Result Rate is a measure of how well it is resonating with the audience it is being shown to. If the result rate is too low, then either the right ad is being shown to the wrong audience, or the wrong ad is being shown to the right audience.

Figuring out which of those is true is a skill that takes time to develop, but I typically start with taking a critical look at my audience selections to see if I was too broad with my choices. If I think that the interests I've picked are bang on, then I'll turn my attention to the ad creative to see if I can improve that (more on that later).

COST PER RESULT

This one is fairly obvious. If the cost per result is too high, then it gets harder for the ad to be profitable.

Exactly how high you can tolerate is something we'll get into when we cover how to calculate the cost of a sale. However, I have some basic guidelines for you (All prices in USD, targeting a US audience—other countries can perform differently).

A hard ceiling is $0.30. An ad that goes above thirty cents for more than a few days needs attention. It could be that the ad has saturated its audience, or maybe the audience isn't quite right, or the creative isn't hitting the mark. The reason will take some examination, but don't let ads linger above $0.30 for too long, because they're cutting into your profitability.

That being said, most ads can do considerably better than $0.30. Contemporary Romance ads should be under $0.20; typically, I like to see them down around $0.15.

Most other major genres should be able to get their ads under $0.20 as well. Niche genres (like my queer/lesbian military science fiction) are hard to get under $0.20, but it is possible.

Personally, I set my ceiling at $0.25 for my ads.

FREQUENCY

This number will usually be somewhere between 1 and 3. It is the average number of times a given human has seen your ad within the date range you've selected.

Generally, when I look at the Frequency, I like to do it over the span of 30 days, which you can set in the date range selector in the upper right of the Ad Manager.

A high Frequency is a good indicator that an ad is saturating its audience, resulting in a low Result Rate and a higher Cost Per Result.

Bringing this metric into the evaluation gives us a lot more insight into what could be going wrong with an ad.

Let's say we have an ad with a 2% result rate.

If it has a low Frequency (under 1.5) over the span of 30 days, we know that it's not saturating its audience, it's just not resonating with them.

However, if it is over 2.5, then it's likely that the ad *has* saturated the audience, and we'll need to change up the creative to re-engage them (or find a new audience).

I rarely alter ads as a result of the Frequency alone. Instead, it's a value I use to determine which action I should take with the ad.

YOUR AD'S FIRST FEW DAYS OF LIFE

Before we get into how to tweak your ad, I want to take just a moment to talk about its early days and what you should expect. Because I don't want you to panic and mess up what could be a great ad.

A HIGH COST PER RESULT

The Cost Per Result (CPR) on an ad is the *average* of what you paid to have someone click on the ad.

I could have an ad that displays a $0.30 CPR on day two, but had a dozen clicks on day one, over $1 each, and have come down into the $0.20 range by day three. The average is unacceptable, but the trend is moving in the right direction.

In short, it's very likely that you'll see a high cost per click at the outset. Only ads that are *amazing* home runs start off with very low CPRs.

This brings us to the...

LEARNING PHASE

When you first create an ad, Facebook selects a large pool of people to show it to. It then pays close attention to the folks who engage with your ad, working to figure out which users will convert the best.

Through this phase, it narrows the audience down from the millions that match your interest selections, to a hundred thousand or less. From testing I've done, it also seems to take the budget into account when creating this smaller sub-audience.

There are some very, very polarized opinions about the learning phase. Some people think that reentering the learning phase brings about ad death.

Others swear their ads only serve well *during* the learning phase, and once it's out of that stage, they kill the ad and make a new one (wow, that sounds exhausting).

Some people also claim that unless you start with a *large* daily budget of at least $50, Facebook will limit your audience so much, the ad is useless.

Still others believe that starting an ad with that high a budget is a great way to confuse the AIs into never finding the right audience to show the ad to.

So which method is right?

The answer is: Yes

All of these methods work, and all of them can fail. However, unless you're willing to light $150 in cash on fire *right now*, don't do the $50/day budget.

I know people who have had success with the method where they kill the ad on day three (when it exits learning) and make a new one. Typically, folks who do this also start with astronomical budgets, and rarely see ROIs higher than 50% (which is to say that for every $100 they spend, they'll get $150 back in royalties/net sales value).

To me, that sounds like a lot of work and a lot of risk (I like neither) for what I'd consider mediocre ROI.

My goal is to work ads toward 100% ROI (doubling my money), and then ultimately toward 200% or higher. In my experience, it takes honing existing ads to achieve that, not shot-gunning new ones at the system.

Again, that depends a lot on how much disposable income you have and what your tolerance for risk is.

I'm of the belief that one can start an ad out at $5/day to prove out its effectiveness before scaling it. We'll get into that in more detail when I go over how to nurture a good ad.

ANALYZING PLACEMENTS

Back when I had you set up the Ad Set, I said to leave "Placements" on automatic (now called "Advantage Placements), which has the ad show up in a host of locations (about 30, give or take a bit).

We go to the "Ad Set" tab for this, because we want to see placements for each Ad Set, whereas if we do it at the campaign level, the values would be an average of all Ad Sets in the campaign.

Click the "Breakdown" button in the upper right and mouse over "By Delivery". A menu will pop out, and you'll need to scroll down a bit to get to "Placements".

The page will expand, and under each Ad Set, we see a list of all locations the ad is showing.

Ad set			Delivery ↑	Reach	Impressions	Budget	Results	Cost per result	Result rate	Frequency
KU Lyeka Authors			● Active	46,192	113,586	$25.00 Daily	6,209 Link Clicks	$0.11 Per Link Click	5.47%	2.46
Facebook	Facebook Reels	Mobile app		448	813		25	$0.14	3.08%	1.81
Facebook	Ads on Facebook Reels	Mobile app		1,864	2,718		70	$0.10	2.58%	1.46
Facebook	Facebook Stories	Mobile app		8	83		4	$0.10	4.82%	10.38
Facebook	Facebook Feed	Desktop		1,536	3,314		191	$0.12	5.76%	2.16
Facebook	Facebook Feed	Mobile app		28,224	70,377		3,864	$0.11	5.50%	2.49
Facebook	Facebook Feed	Mobile web		64	111		2	$0.12	1.80%	1.73
Facebook	Marketplace	Desktop		312	540		23	$0.11	4.26%	1.73
Facebook	Marketplace	Mobile app		10,680	20,606		1,564	$0.11	7.59%	1.93
Facebook	Right column	Desktop		2,296	8,060		66	$0.11	0.82%	3.51
Facebook	Search results	Desktop			1		–	–	–	–
Facebook	Search results	Mobile app		30	30		3	$0.08	10.00%	1.00
Facebook	Feed: video feeds	Desktop		80	140		2	$0.19	1.43%	1.76
Facebook	Feed: video feeds	Mobile app		4,056	6,740		380	$0.09	5.64%	1.66
Instagram	Instagram Reels	Mobile app		8	29		5	$0.10	17.24%	3.63
Instagram	Instagram Stories	Mobile app		16	24		5	$0.13	20.83%	1.50

Not all of these locations will get good action, as we can see in the Impressions column. The place your ad will likely show the most is the Facebook Feed on the Mobile App. Desktop feed is usually second, but in this ad's case, it's the Right Column on Desktop.

What I'm doing here is looking for locations where the ad is underperforming. I start by looking at the CPR, using my Mobile Feed value as the benchmark. Here, it is $0.12, so I'm looking for locations that cost more. Interestingly, none are higher, so I'm unlikely to nix any.

You may wonder about placements like Reels or Right Column. They have result rates below my normal thresholds. That's okay, though, because the numbers I gave earlier were for the Ad Set's averages. Some placements do better, others do worse. If a placement (say, Facebook Reels) had a CPR of $0.18 *and* that low 1.20% Result Rate, I would probably remove the placement. However, if it had a CPR of $0.18 and a Result Rate of 7%, I would probably keep it, because the RR is so much higher than the Mobile Feed's.

While there's no hard science here, I personally use a rule of thirds. If a placement's CPR is one third higher than the Mobile Feed (or goes above my personal hard limit of $0.25), then I consider nuking it.

However, if its Result Rate is one third *better* than the Mobile Feed's (which means the RR is higher), I will probably let the placement slide.

ASSESSMENT EXAMPLE

The Mobile Feed has a $0.15 CPR and 5% Result Rate.

If Facebook Reels has a CPR of $0.21, that is a third again higher than the Mobile Feed's. That's not an insignificant increase in cost. However, if its result rate is over 7%, I may let it stick around. That's sort of on the cusp, though. An RR of 9% would make it a guarantee.

The reason is the high Result Rate makes me think that people who click are more engaged, and thus, more likely to buy.

As an example, if a person viewing the Mobile Feed has a 1 in 20 chance of buying, that means it will cost me $3.00 (20 x $0.15) to sell the book.

However, if the person viewing the Reel has a one in 10 chance of buying, it only costs $2.10 to sell book 1, even though the CPR is $0.06 higher.

REMOVING PLACEMENTS

Should a placement not pass muster, you'll want to edit the Ad Set (mouse over its name in the list and choose "edit").

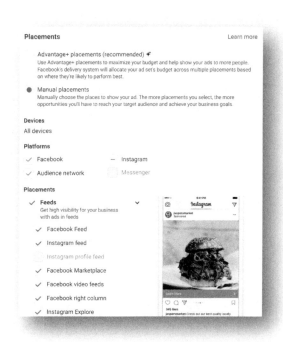

Scroll to the bottom of the page where the "Placements" section lives (it may be the last or second to last section, depending on which version of the Ad Manager you have). Switch the setting from "Automatic Placements" (which may say something like "Advantage Placement", like mine does).

The full list of placements will open up, and the underperforming placement can be removed.

When I first make an ad, I look at the placements after seven days to see if there are any stinkers. Then I'll look again in a couple of weeks, and finally, a month or so out. After that, it's unlikely that any further pruning is necessary.

When you're done, click "Breakdown" again, and choose "Clear Breakdowns" to remove the clutter from the page.

ANALYZING CREATIVE

If you've chosen to use Dynamic Creative (which I do every single time), or if you've added more than one Primary Text or Headline option, we'll need to perform the same analysis on those items as we did on the Placements.

To do this, go to the ad tab for the ad you wish to examine. Once there, click the "Breakdown" button in the upper right, this time selecting "By Dynamic Creative Element".

Sometimes, even if you have dynamic elements, this selection is greyed out. If that happens, refresh the page, and it should become available.

Here, we're going to perform the same analysis on "Image, video and slideshow", "Text", and "Headline" as we did on the placements in the section above. Though, there is a caveat: in these scenarios, there's nothing analogous to the Mobile Feed that we can use to compare.

Instead, we're going to have to establish our own acceptable mean. Here's how I do it.

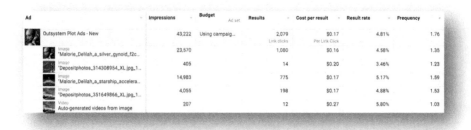

Ad	Impressions	Budget Ad set	Results	Cost per result	Result rate	Frequency
Outsystem Plot Ads - New	43,222	Using campaig...	2,079 Link clicks	$0.17 Per Link Click	4.81%	1.76
Image "Malorie_Delilah_a_silver_gynoid_f2c..	23,570		1,080	$0.16	4.58%	1.35
Image "Depositphotos_314308954_XL.jpg_1..	405		14	$0.20	3.46%	1.23
Image "Malorie_Delilah_a_starship_accelera..	14,983		775	$0.17	5.17%	1.59
Image "Depositphotos_351649866_XL.jpg_1..	4,055		198	$0.17	4.88%	1.53
Video Auto-generated videos from image	207		12	$0.27	5.80%	1.03

First, I look at the number of impressions and results an option has received. Ideally, we should have over 100 impressions of an image (or text element) to be able to judge its performance.

Make sure you've selected a date range of at least 30 days in the upper right of the Ad Manager.

Look at the images (or other creative element) that have received the most impressions and have the most results. These are the ones that Facebook is preferring to show and are utilizing the bulk of my budget.

In this case, it's the first and third image, with the first getting the lion's share of the impressions and most of the clicks.

Analysis Mindset Divergence!

On the Ad Set page, if you are able to set when you are charged to "Link Click (CPC)" and not "Impression", then we are less concerned with creative elements that get a lot of impressions but not too many clicks, as we don't pay by impression.

However, if you *are* paying by impression, an under-performing element that has boatloads of impressions and not a lot of clicks is costing you money.

Luckily, this is represented in our result rate, so we don't have to look too closely at that, but it's something to keep in mind.

On the example above, it's interesting to note that Facebook is preferring image #1, even though it's significantly more expensive than #3. Normally, the system doesn't do this, but if it does, the reason is typically because the image has a better result rate.

But in this case, #3 has a better CPR *and* a better Result Rate.

Well, shucks. What now?

Let's take a closer look at these two images.

They are *wildly different*. One is an image of a strange robotic woman, while the other is of what looks like a spaceship blasting out of atmosphere with a blooming explosion below.

I can bet that one of these images will appeal to you more than the other. It could be the content and composition, or it could be the color palette.

Because I turned on "Optimize Creative For Each Person" on my ad, I can assume that Facebook is picking the right image for a given person based on their previous activity on other posts and ads.

Moreover, the ad showing the woman may have a lower Result Rate and higher CPR because it just gets shown so darn much and the same people may be seeing it more. This supposition is confirmed by it having a higher Frequency.

Still, $0.06 more is a lot. I'm on the fence about that picture, but I don't want to simply remove it, because what if it is generating the majority of my sales, and the other images won't perform as well when put in front of the masses that previously saw the silver woman?

I might want to test out some changes, which I'll discuss in the next section.

Setting aside the issue of one of the most expensive images getting the lion's share of the action, I at least now have a benchmark. A mean CPR between the two most popular images is about $0.15, and they prove that I can get a 4% Result Rate. I'll accept some deviation, but not too much.

Image #2 stands out, with its 1.85% Result Rate. It has low CPR and it's not getting a lot of action, so I'm not in a rush to yeet it from the ad. However, toward the bottom are two other offenders.

(Above: image #2 and #4 in the dynamic creative breakdown)

Image #4 has a pretty high CPR ($0.18), but its Result Rate (3.87%) isn't one third again below the mean of the #1 and #3's result rates (about 4.25%).

I'll probably let it slide.

These two images are underperforming, though in different ways. The reason I picked them out to begin with is I liked the art style, and they had some level of blueness to them and I like a variety of color options.

What I really need to do is find a better blue image and swap it in. I only have four images, so I could probably just add a fifth into the mix, but given the cost of #4, I'll probably vote it off the island and try to find something better.

WHAT'S WITH THIS VIDEO?

If you've chosen to use Dynamic Creative, you'll often see a video at the bottom of the images and video breakdown. Chances are that you didn't add a video of your own, so Facebook made this one out of the provided images. Sometimes it makes a slideshow, other times it takes one image and slowly zooms in to create the illusion of motion.

Sometimes Facebook nails it, and the video is the best performing thing on the list. Other times, it *bombs*.

Given that, over the course of three months (in this particular case), Facebook has only managed to secure four clicks on the image, I'm going to say this one is participating in the aforementioned bombing.

The fact that it has the lowest Result Rate and the highest CPR in the list seals its fate.

However, we didn't add this video, so we can't just remove it. What to do?

One option is to do nothing. Given the low number of impressions this image has, it's clear that Facebook has given up showing it. If the video were being served a lot more frequently and getting a bunch of expensive clicks, I'd be more motivated to toss it into the harbor.

For the sake of an example, let's say I have decided to axe the video. One way to do that is to remove the video placements on the Ad Set.

The other is to change up the images on the ad itself. Usually, that will prompt Facebook to create a new video with the updated creative.

Since I want to find another blue-tinted image for this ad anyway, that's the route I'll take—we'll walk through those steps shortly.

TEXT ELEMENTS

The other things we'll want to take a look at is the text options, both the "Primary Text" (which is just labeled "text" in the breakdown), and the "Headline" (which has an unnecessary parenthetical after it).

I apply the same analysis to these text elements as I do to the images, following the same process.

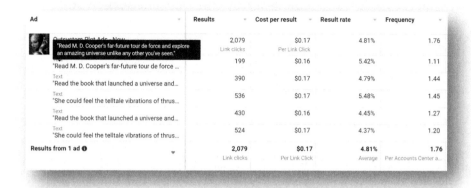

To help figure out which text option is which, you can mouse over them on the left and see the full text.

One thing you may notice is that your headlines are in the text section *and* in the headline section. The reason for this is Facebook will test your headlines both above and below the image.

In this example, the item I've highlighted is one of my headlines. Interestingly, it has a *great* Result Rate, though its CPR leaves something to be desired. Still, it's not much worse than that of the text Facebook is showing the most.

There's nothing we can do about the headlines on the text section, so I tend to analyze them in their section and decide there which to keep, letting that decision trickle through to the instances where they get shown above the fold.

Corner Case

It can sometimes happen that a headline does great when it's shown in the Primary Text spot, but not when it's shown as a headline.

In that scenario, I remove it from the Headline section and add it as a Primary Text option.

THE DEVIL IS IN THE DETAILS

Some of you may have noticed that the silver woman and the third text option (which is a snippet of the book's first chapter) both have over 30,000 impressions. What that tells us is that they are shown together *a lot*.

This is confirmed by their near-identical CPR and Result Rates.

This means a change to one will change the other. If you're being careful in your testing and trying not to turn too many knobs at once, keep an eye out for patterns like that, and only change one *or* the other (if you choose to change them at all).

A SEGUE INTO SOCIAL PROOF

"Social Proof" is a term used to describe the effect of comments, likes, and shares on your ad. Since it's impossible for Facebook (or any other social media platform, for that matter) to determine the veracity and quality of an ad and its products, they utilize the reactions of their users to assess an ad.

Specifically, social proof actions help to measure the engagement quality of the ad, but that is far from the extent of the benefit that comments, likes, and shares provide.

The biggest benefit is the psychological effect that it has on other folks who see the ad. Just like reviews on a book, the more comments and likes (and shares, to a lesser extent) that an ad has, the more likely people are to trust what it says (so long as the comments are neutral or positive).

This is one of the reasons it's ideal not to make too many variations of an ad: it helps keep the social proof from being diluted across too many ads.

Warning: certain changes to your ad can cause Facebook to remove the social proof.

Any element in the "Ad Creative" box on the Ad itself cannot be changed, lest Facebook remove all comments, likes, and shares from the post. They do this because bad actors will build up social proof on one ad and then leverage that to advertise multiple products.

There have been instances where I fixed small grammatical issues in the ad copy and *didn't* lose my social proof, but I don't know where the threshold is for its removal, so be careful.

TESTING OUT AD CHANGES

Let's start with Dynamic Creative ads.

If you recall what I said earlier, Facebook essentially creates every possible combination of your ad's images, Primary Text, and headlines.

That means 5 images, 3 Primary Text options, and 2 headlines comes to 30 possible combinations.

That being said, Facebook doesn't waste a lot of time showing all of those, and quickly weeds out combos that don't work well.

Ad		Impressions	Results	Cost per result	Result rate	Frequency
Outsystem Plot Ads - New ✏️ 📊 View charts ✏️ Edit 📋 Duplicate 📌 Pin		38,900	1,594 Link clicks	$0.17 Per Link Click	4.10%	2.05
	Image "Malorie_Delilah_a_silver_gynoid_f2c...	30,685	1,254	$0.18	4.09%	1.85
	Image "Depositphotos_314308954_XL.jpg_1...	917	17	$0.13	1.85%	1.59
	Image "Malorie_Delilah_a_starship_accelera...	6,556	296	$0.12	4.51%	1.45
	Image "Depositphotos_351649866_XL.jpg_1...	595	23	$0.18	3.87%	1.63
	Video Auto-generated videos from image	147	4	$0.19	2.72%	1.17

Referring back to my image breakdown, we can see that three of these images have been used fewer than 1000 times. Given that there are three Primary Text options and two headlines on this ad, chances are that no single combination using these images has been viewed more than 500 times.

What that means is there is likely very little social proof on those images. Because of that, I'll generally just pop into the ad and delete those images (or text elements, if one of those is the underperforming item).

To do this, simply edit the ad, scroll down to the image or text you wish to delete, click the little X and then publish the ad to push the changes live.

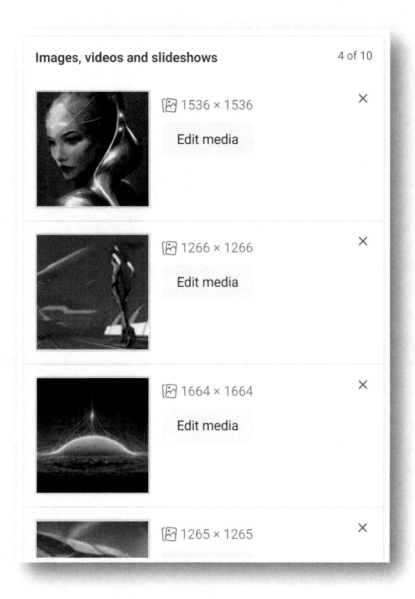

Doing so will remove any variation of the ad using that element (and thus remove its social proof), but leave all other variations intact.

DO I REPLACE OR REMOVE?

I could hear you asking that question from here. The answer depends on how many elements there are. I like to give Facebook at least 3 images, 2 Primary Text options, and 2 headlines. If I dip below that number, then I'll add new ones to meet that threshold again.

Sometimes I'll endeavor to keep an ad up at 5 images, if it's high spend (over $20/day), because I don't want to saturate the audience with the same images over and over.

The selection process is a bit of an art, and can depend on a lot of factors, but keep in mind that our goal is ultimately to have enough creative in an ad that, over a 30-day period, our Frequency doesn't rise too high over 2 for any given element (though the entire ad in aggregate can go up to 2.5 without concern).

Our other goal is to get a set of solid performers in our ad so that we can basically ignore it as much as possible and get back to writing (or whatever else you may have to do that doesn't involve babysitting ads).

Once you have the new element(s) in place, then we're back to checking every 5 – 10 days until we know it's solid. The same analysis as above applies.

DON'T TURN TOO MANY KNOBS AT ONCE

No one has a crystal ball (well, I do, but it's in need of repairs, on account of it not working), and no one knows for sure which ads will work best.

There are thousands of variables that can affect how well your ad is going to perform. If you're like me, you don't have time (or patience, or perhaps money) to test thousands of changes. Even testing five or six different variables (multivariate testing) is exponential. For example, if you have two sets of five variables (five pieces of text and five images), you have 25 possible combinations to test. Changing that many things at once means you'll have to wait weeks or more to see which are working.

Nuts! Ain't *nobody* got time for that!

This is where multivariate testing's little brother, A/B testing, comes into play.

Rather than change a host of items, you take a SWAG (scientific, wild-assed guess) at the biggest variable, and try two versions of the ad, with the only difference being that *one* element.

I'll give you a hint: that biggest variable is invariably the image (see what I did there?).

The image is going to make or break your ad before anyone reads a single word of the copy, so that's what we want to twiddle with first.

If we harken back to my image conundrum (that Facebook is serving the silver woman the most, even though she's more expensive than other options), that's the thing I want to test. Namely, I want to remove that image and put in some other options (two at most) to see if I can get the lower-cost images to serve more often.

But what if that test fails? Given that the vast majority of my impressions have been on the version(s) of my ad showing the sliver woman, if I remove her, I've nuked my social proof and I don't know if my change will work…

Cue nail biting!

DUPE THAT AD!

Fear not! There is a solution for this. Duplication.

If you are using Dynamic Creative, you have to dupe at the Ad Set level, as they can only have one Ad in each Ad Set. If you are not using DC, you can dupe at the ad level, but just remember that if you do so, both ads will pull from the same budget, and if that is at $5/day, it may take some time to have enough data regarding the efficacy of the change.

Conversely, if you dupe at the Ad Set level, remember that each Ad Set has its own budget and you run the risk of spending more money than you intended.

As an example, if you have an Ad Set at $20/day and you want to test out a change, peel off $5 from its budget and put it into the new variation. Then you can see how that one works without jeopardizing an ad that is likely (if it's performing well) making you $30-$50/day.

Another option is to use "Campaign Budget Optimization", which will allocate budget to Ad Sets based on which are currently performing well.

A final budget-conserving option is to pause the original ad while you test out the new version. Facebook ads aren't like AMS ads; a paused ad can be turned back on without it failing to serve or perform how it did in the past, though it may go through a brief (1-3 day) learning phase.

Whether you choose to duplicate the Ad or Ad Set, the process is the same. Mouse over the row for the item, and a link that says "Duplicate" will appear.

On a smaller screen, you may not see the word, just the icon. It looks a little like two pieces of paper, overlapped.

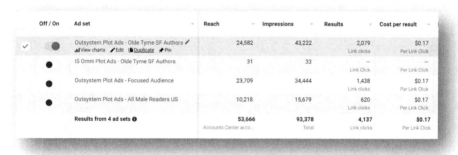

Once you click that, a window will pop up. I typically don't change any options, as I keep all my ads for a given book/series in the same campaign. I also (usually) only want one copy, so I don't change that.

Lastly, leave the box at the bottom checked, as that will preserve the social proof on variations we're not changing.

DEMOGRAPHICS AND PERFORMANCE

I imagine you've picked up by now how I'm big on testing and using data to determine whether something is working. I believe that knowing when something is *not* working is the most important of the two.

We only have so much time, money, and effort available to us in life, so we need to spend as little of all three on endeavors that don't serve us.

Luckily, Facebook gives us oodles of information to help find out what those are.

VISUAL AIDS!

Facebook has some handy dandy charts available to help analyze ads. Most of this data can be found by using breakdowns, but some of us are more visual, so these can be helpful.

Just as we did in the previous section on duplicating, mouse over the item you wish to examine and click "View Charts".

PERFORMANCE OVERVIEW

The first chart is the Performance Overview. This graph used to be better than it is now (in that you used to be able to view multiple metrics on the same chart), but it's still serviceable.

5/31/2023

This graph (like everything else in the Ad Manager) shows data for the date range selected in the upper right of the screen, so if you'd like to see more historical data, be sure to adjust the date range.

This particular image also a really good example of how the performance of an unchanged ad can wax and wane over the months. Clearly visible here is the Late October Effect (traditional publishers release up to 80% of their catalog in October), the American Thanksgiving Effect (which didn't hit this ad too much), and the Post-Christmas Spike.

So long as the spend has remained constant, we'll see the inverse of this graph when we look at the Per Link Click numbers (since the more the clicks cost, the fewer of them our fixed budget can afford).

Examining these numbers is useful for identifying trends. If this ad's CPR had continued to rise during and following Christmas, then I would have considered making a change to it.

The third default metric is the "CTR (all)". This is similar, but not completely analogous to, the Result Rate. CTR (all) contains *all* clicks, including ones going to your page, the "read more" link, and literally anything else that can be clicked.

Even so, it's a handy for spotting the trends. Though the values are different, the CTR (all) trend will mostly mirror that of the Result Rate.

There are a few other metrics one can examine via charts (but not Result Rate! *shakes fist at Meta*), though I don't find many to be all that useful.

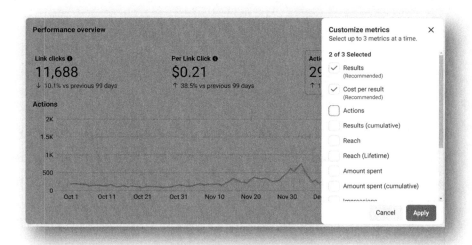

To view other metrics, click the "Customize Metrics" button in the upper right. You'll need to uncheck one of the three default metrics in order to enable another.

One that is kinda neat is the "Actions" metric. This shows the daily number of actions on the ad. Those essentially include all social proof actions, plus clicks. It makes for a great measure of how well engagement on your ad is doing.

Interestingly, there seems to be more engagement around holidays. Since the clicks didn't spike quite as much as the actions, I have to assume that when people have more time, they engage more (just a guess).

Either way, it looks like this ad still has legs.

Another metric I find useful is "Reach". This shows how many new humans the ad is being seen by.

If the line begins to plateau, that means Facebook isn't finding a lot of new people to show it to. If that occurs, it's time to find new people, either by changing the Ad Set audience, or spiking the spend to force Meta to put the ad back in the learning phase, which should uncover new folks to show it to.

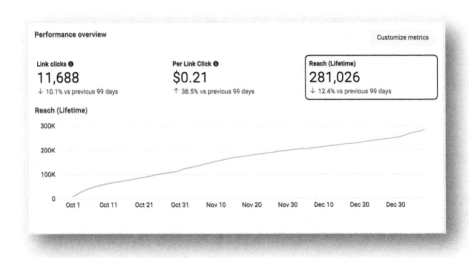

Another number that complements the Reach metric is Frequency.

It's useful to see this graphed out over time, as it shows whether the same people are seeing the ad. If the Reach is climbing at a steady pace, then the Frequency should be relatively flat—which is what we see in the chart below.

You'll also note that the slight dip in Frequency following the holidays mirrors the bump in the reach chart for the same timeframe.

What this tells me is that an ad that has been running since June 8th is continuing to find a new audience, so I have no reason to turn it off or adjust it—as long as it's selling books on the retailers.

For those interested, here is a longer view of the ad's performance. I increased spend in early August to combat the end of summer slump. It'll be interesting to see if the upward trend continues through January.

WAIT...WHY IS FACEBOOK TELLING ME THIS?

Often, you'll get recommendations below the Performance Overview graph. Sometimes these are useful, but usually they aren't.

Here's one that popped up while I was taking these screenshots:

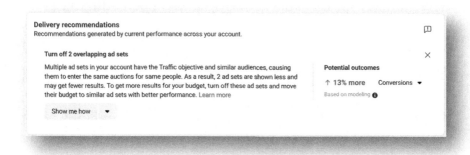

Take those suggestions with a grain of salt. Facebook doesn't understand your personal goals, it only considers its own ultimate goal of separating you from your money.

Despite my cynical outlook, Meta really is trying to save me some cash with this one. However, I *know* I'm advertising to the same audience. All my audiences have some measure of overlap, since I mostly write Science Fiction books.

In this particular case, the audiences in question have *complete* overlap because I'm testing creative options, and I want to do that with the same audience. So following this particular recommendation would terminate my test.

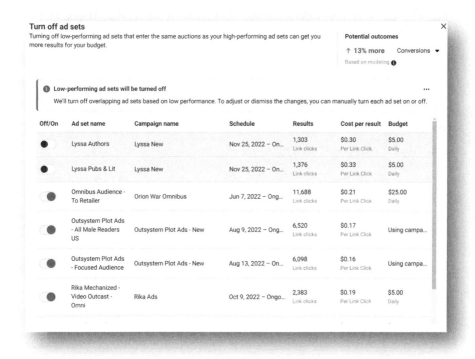

To be fair, the ads it advises I turn off are way over my thresholds. There's a sad tale behind them that can be summed up as an accidental deletion, and for some reason, I can't get the new ones to perform as well as the old ones.

This is super rare, but it does happen.

Don't be a Malorie. Don't delete your ads. And if you do, be *super careful* about what items might be selected when you hit that delete button.

If you're curious why I'm letting ads with such terrible CPRs run, it's because I'm trying to dig into the *why* behind these ads performing so poorly after I recreated them to be identical to the originals.

Thus far, I think it's because I remade them on Black Friday, and the pool of people to show them to was so small that I got a bum audience.

Because January 1st is a day when most people are doing pretty much nothing at all, I adjusted the audience on December 31st to see if I could put it back in the learning phase and find a new audience.

As you can see, it worked, and the Frequency post-change dropped to about 1.29. The CPR is still higher than I'd like, but no longer breaching my thresholds.

DEMOGRAPHICS

We can view demographics for an entire Ad Set, or just for an ad. If you use Dynamic Creative, you can look at this at either the Ad or Ad Set level.

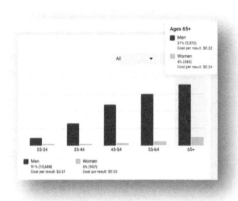

If you are not using DC and have more than one Ad in an Ad Set, then you'll want to analyze the Ad level.

Typically, I recommend not running ads to both men and women at once, as one usually outperforms the other and it is often not worth the cost to advertise to both.

That being said, some genres do equally well advertising to men and women. Still, the audiences are often different sizes, so I prefer to run separate ads so I can tune the spend based on those variables.

Traditional Science Fiction novels are notoriously hard to advertise to women (despite many women liking them) for a host of reasons that require a segue far beyond the bounds of this book's purpose, so I'll leave my lamenting for a different medium.

PART 7: THE VALUE OF A SALE

Now that we have ads running, it's time to examine their profitability.

Chances are, you have a number of activities that drive people to your book pages on various retailers. Those probably include new releases, paid promos, swaps, newsletters, AMS (Amazon) ads, Facebook ads, and perhaps even Pinterest and BookBub ads.

Add to that word of mouth sales, and it can be exceedingly difficult to determine which channel is best contributing to your sales volume.

Up until very recently, we had to do a lot of guesswork make a swag at this, but in October of 2022, Amazon released a tool for authors called "Attribution Tags".

These allow us to make special links to our books and then get reports that show how many books were sold, as well as how many KU page reads we got from the ad.

Granted, this only works for sales on Amazon, but that is significantly more information than we had before. It is *far and away* better than using affiliate links in an attempt to gauge sales.

AMAZON ATTRIBUTION LINKS

To access the Attribution Tags system, go to your AMS dashboard. If you're not sure how to get there, open up your KDP Bookshelf, click the "Marketing" link in the top menu.

On the next page, there is a section labeled "Amazon Ads". To start, choose the Amazon.com marketplace and then click "Go to Ads Console".

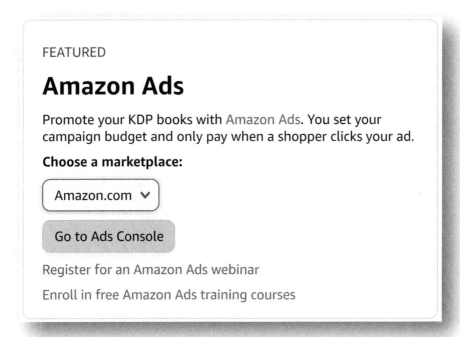

That will take you to the Amazon Ads dashboard. Once there, mouse over the little graph icon on the left, and click "Amazon Attribution".

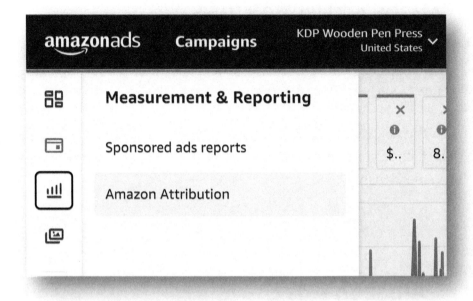

That will bring you to the glorious Attribution Tags Console!

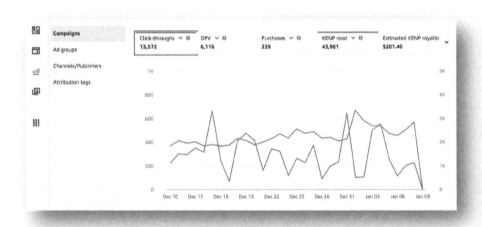

Here, you will see a graph for all of the tracking you have set up. The default will show how many clicks have come in and how many KU reads you've gotten.

It will only show two items at once, so you'll have to turn off Click-Throughs or KENP to see sales or other data. Also, when you load any new page, it will revert to these two metrics and also reset the date range to the last 30 days. Keep an eye on that when you're going over stats, or you'll drive yourself mad trying to make sense of the numbers.

To begin with, you'll need to make campaigns here that mirror the campaigns you intend to make in Facebook.

Personally, I make a campaign for each book/series I advertise, so I also make campaigns for each series I have in the Attribution Tags system.

To do this, click the blue "Create Campaign" button below the chart. The next page will ask if you wish to create a campaign manually or upload a file.

Choose "Create Manually".

A section will then appear providing fields to make the campaign and ad groups.

Enter the Campaign Name (again, match this to the campaign name in Facebook— usually a book or series name).

Below that, there is a section to select the books you wish to track. I select each book in the series, because if I show an ad for book 1, and someone buys another book in the series as a result of clicking on the ad, I want to know that.

Search for the books in the series (this search is case sensitive) and add them all (I add both the ebooks and print versions).

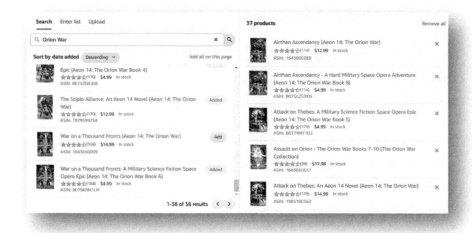

Once you've done that, scroll down to the "Ad Groups" section. I make a group for each Ad Set I've made in the Meta Ad Manager. Since I prefer Dynamic Creative ads, there is only one Ad in an Ad Set.

If you choose not to use Dynamic Creative and instead made multiple ads inside the Ad Set, then you will need to make an Ad Group in the Attribution tag system for each Ad in Facebook.

In short, if you use Dynamic Creative, then implement a 1 to 1 relationship between:

- Attribution Tag Campaigns and Facebook/Meta Campaigns

- Attribution Tag Ad Groups and Facebook/Meta Ad **Sets**

If you do not use Dynamic Creative, then implement a 1 to 1 relationship between:

- Attribution Tag Campaigns and Facebook/Meta Campaigns
- Attribution Tag Ad Groups and Facebook/Meta **Ads**

In the "Ad Group name" field, put in the Ad Set or Ad name from Ad Manager. Choose Facebook from "Publisher" and Social from "Channel". These don't really matter much, but are handy for reporting by where ads are showing if you use multiple platforms.

The final field is the page you want the reader to go to on Amazon after they click the link. This can be either the product details page for the book being advertised or the series page.

As discussed elsewhere in this book, sometimes one performs better than the other, and it can be useful to test them both.

Be sure that you use a nice clean link to your product page, using the **https://amazon.com/dp/ASIN** format (series pages also have an ASIN, and the nine-digit ISBN is the ASIN for print books).

Create as many Ad Groups as necessary (you can add more later if needed) and then click the blue "Create" button in the upper right corner of the page.

A page will load that looks something like this:

The link under the "Attribution Tags" column is the link you'll use in your ad. If it's tricky to copy it off the page, you can download the CSV file from the link toward the top of the page.

Elsewhere in this book, I recommend also putting the links to your book at the bottom of the Primary Text when making your ad. But obviously, you don't want to put these big ugly links there.

I recommend using Bitly to shorten the links. They have an agreement with Amazon that allows them to make amzn.to links, which Facebook sees as Amazon links, not a redirect service.

ANALYZING THE ATTRIBUTION TAG DATA

It will take about a week after creating an ad that's using attribution tag links to reflect a useful volume of data in the system. At that point, though, you should have enough to start assessing things.

Note: Amazon's system uses a 14-day attribution. That means that if someone clicks a link on your ad today but doesn't buy the book for another two weeks, the ad will still be credited.

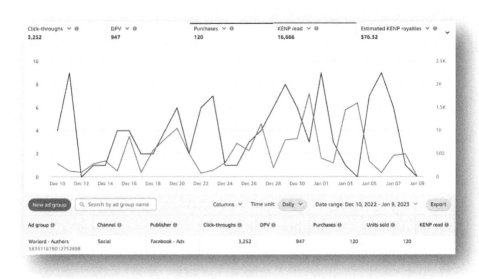

It does lag a bit in populating sales, so I tend to not make drastic decisions based on the past 3-5 days.

The screenshot below shows the sales and reads for the past thirty days. While my testing has shown that the tracking system misses 1/3 of the sales and 2/3 of the reads, I like to use the data on the page for my initial assessment.

I start with sales and then look at KU.

Over the past thirty days, the system reports 3,252 clicks and 120 sales. If I want to learn how many clicks it takes to make a sale, I divide the clicks by the sales.

$$3252 \div 120$$
$$= 27.1$$

A sale every 27 clicks isn't amazing, but it's not terrible, either. However, there is a bit more to dig into. Remember how I put every book in the series in the tracking? Some of those 120 sales are probably for books 2 and 3.

On the upper left, there is a link for Products. Clicking on this will break down the sales by book. It will show other books people looked at after clicking the link in your ad, to make it easier to parse, click the "Purchases" column header to get it to sort by number of purchases. You may have to click it twice to get the largest number on top.

With this new breakdown, we see that there were only 71 sales of book 1. In that light, it's taking 45 clicks to sell book 1. That's not quite as good, but I'm not looking at KU yet, so there's hope yet for this ad's profitability.

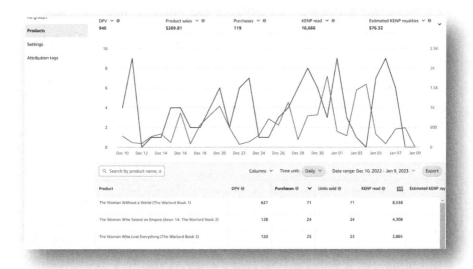

Like I mentioned before, the tracking system misses about 1/3 of the sales.

This particular series was entirely dead before I fired up ads for it, selling about two books a month. Because of this, I can be fairly certain that nearly every sale of this book comes from the ads.

The KDP Dashboard shows 111 sales of book 1 during the same period.

$$3252 \div 111$$

$$= 29.3$$

Well, that looks better! I can breathe a sigh of relief.

The next thing I need to figure out is how much each sale of book 1 is costing me. Checking the Ads Manager shows that my average CPR over the past 30 days is $0.20.

You may notice that the clicks (called "Results" in Ad Manager) are fewer here than in the Attribution Tags system. Often, the clicks reported in the two systems don't line up.

This can happen for a host of reasons, from a difference in time zone where the calculations are being done (Facebook is GMT, and Amazon is PST), to different methods for de-duping* clicks.

*De-duping means removing duplicate clicks that can be caused by people clicking twice in close succession and a few other similar situations.

With that in mind, the most generous calculation would be to use the 3,015 results from Ad Manager, not the 3,252 in the Attribution Tags system. I generally feel okay doing that because the number in Meta is the number of clicks I'm paying for.

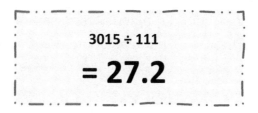

3015 ÷ 111

= 27.2

Coincidentally, that brings me back to almost the same place as the original calculation I made for number of clicks to make a sale.

I went through all of this to show a few different ways of looking at the same numbers, and to show the rationale for the way I do it.

The final calculation here is to multiply my CPR of $0.20 by the number of clicks it takes to sell the book.

27.2 x $0.20

= $5.44

Alright! There it is, this is my cost to sell book 1. By the by, if I use the least forgiving numbers from the calculations above (the 29.3 clicks to make a sale), I wind up with $5.86 to sell book 1.

Using my readthrough calculations, the value of my sales with readthrough is only $3.27, which means I'm losing money. However, the books are in KU, and with that readthrough, the value comes to $6.10.

That's somewhat better. I'm not losing money, but I'm not doing great, either. I'm making about $0.60 whenever I sell book 1.

I must say, there's a reason this series was dead. It has really bad readthrough, so I don't promote it. If you're curious why, it's the darkest series I've written, where the MC becomes the villain and kills her lover.

Let me tell you... that *nukes* readthrough.

The series is three books long, which is often the bare minimum for Facebook ads to be profitable. I roughed out what I would make if the series was five books long, and the full readthrough value comes to $9.26.

If I were to add two more books, I'd make $3.82 profit when I sell book 1.

As another exercise, I mapped out what it would look like if I hadn't written a series with such bad readthrough *and* had taken it to five books.

That number is $11.09. In that case, I'd be making $5.65 every time I sell book 1.

I think it's useful to see how writing a longer series with good readthrough can take an ad that is just barely profitable and bump it up to doubling my money.

Luckily, I have 124 other books in an interconnected universe, so even if I'm not making much on this series, I make it up when folks move on to the rest of Aeon 14.

A FINAL EXERCISE

Small changes in ad cost can make a pretty big difference with profitability. In the scenario above, imagine that my average CPR was $0.15, not $0.20.

In that situation, we would be looking at 27.2 clicks at $0.15 to sell book 1.

$$27.2 \times \$0.15 = \$4.08$$

That's a pretty big change. I'd go from making $0.60 a sale to $2.02 a sale, which is moving toward a respectable profit.

Let's say I honed my product detail page further, testing out different blurbs to increase conversion. Perhaps I could get my ratio to only 18 clicks to make a sale (I have seen books get down to 6 clicks to make a sale, so this isn't unreasonable at all).

$$18 \times \$0.15 = \$2.70$$

Neither of these values are half what the current numbers are, but the profitability is now at the point where I'm doubling my money!

Now, imagine that this series had better readthrough and five books. That value was $11.09. With a cost to sell of $2.70, that's $8.39 in pure profit, quadrupling my money.

This is why I have some series over ten books, with very good readthrough. Those flagship series earn thousands of dollars on just a few hundred dollars ad spend each month.

A LITTLE ASIDE ON PRICING

The debate on pricing will probably go on forever, and there are as many opinions as there are authors. However, when it comes down to it, there are some key principles at play:

1. People buy things more readily if they are priced lower.
2. People value things more if they spent more money on them.
3. Books that are free, or $0.99, can attract readers who are not your core demographic (because they'll take a chance and buy on a whim, when they may not have at a $3.99 or $4.99 price).
4. Lower-priced books often get more bad reviews because of #3 above. Folks that are on the fence about your plot, character, or premise may buy anyway just to give it a shot. Then they find out it's not their cup of tea, and give a bad review.

> You catch more flies with honey than vinegar.
>
> This is to say that every single one of us has a massive, untapped market. I saw the other day that someone did the math on J. K. Rowling's sales and determined that she had probably only reached 15% of her target demographic.
>
> This means that there are untold *millions* of readers for your book who have not yet seen it. And they're *more likely* to see it if it is priced lower, and ranked higher as a result of more sales and borrows.

What do *I* do, you ask?

I often (though not always) price my first in series books at $0.99, because I want *readers* more than I want money. Because if readers like your stories, they give you more money!

However, you need more books for them to read in order for loss-leader pricing on book 1 to work, so don't drop that price till you have 4-5 books out at the minimum.

PART 8: SCALING ADS

After you've done all the hard work of getting that ad tuned and performing well, you want it to keep on chugging...and maybe even get better and better, right?

Right?

I thought so. Sure, you can have a little ad trickling along at $5/day and help keep a series afloat. I've run some ads for folks with that spend, and they can maintain a series with a $0.99 first book at about the 40,000 – 60,000 rank range.

That's not too bad. If your series is five books long, and you have good read-through, that rank range means you're probably making $10-$30 a day (if you're in KU). Even if only $10 a day of that is coming from ads, you're doubling your money every day.

Very few investments will yield returns like that.

But let's see if we can turn that knob up to 11, shall we?

MANAGING YOUR AD SPEND

You've diligently run your ad at $5/day to get that nice CPR and Result Rate. It has comments and shares, showing social proof. Not only that, but you've used Amazon Attribution Tags to confirm it is making sales.

Now it's time to bump up that spend and make some magic!

Not so fast!

Here's the thing you need to consider: the audience you picked is only so big. At a higher spend rate, your ad may saturate that audience, and Facebook may start charging you a lot more per click because people start hiding your ad, or ignoring it.

You can see this reflected in the Frequency score on your ad. For Dynamic Ads, 1.5 – 2.0 is good; if you're over 2.5, you're starting to saturate the audience. For non-dynamic ads, the threshold is about 2.0, with 1.3 – 1.8 being ideal.

The reason for this is that a DC ad has a lot of ads inside it, so in aggregate, they've been seen more, even though individual combinations have not.

If you really want to drill down with a DC ad, look at the Frequency of your most-shown image. If that's over 2.0, then that image is starting to saturate its audience.

I know what you're thinking: *we already went over all this, why is it an issue again?*

The reason we're refreshing ourselves here is because when it comes to scaling ads, we need headroom.

Let's say we have two Dynamic Creative ads.

Ad One's Stats:
    CPR - $0.16
    Result Rate - 7%
    Frequency of 2.5

Ad Two's Stats:
    CPR - $0.17
    Result Rate - 6.8%
    Frequency of 1.7

On the surface, Ad One looks better, but Ad Two is right behind it, insofar as CPR and Result Rate are concerned.

One thing we know is that as we increase the spend on this ad, the CPR will go up, and the Result Rate will go down. The main factor controlling how much those change will be the Frequency. If it is low, that means we have headroom in the audience, while a high Frequency means we could start to run out of inexpensive targets before long.

We've brushed against this before, but I know the question brewing in your mind:

> *But, Malorie…my audience is 3 million! How can I be exhausting that already?*

Great question! Let's dig into that.

AUDIENCE SIZE AND EXHAUSTION

There are three primary factors that affect how much of your audience your ad will show to.

These are: Competition, Interest Level, Ad Learning Limit.

We'll start with Competition. This is the term I use to describe whether a given person is in the pool of people you can afford to advertise to at any given moment.

It will come as no surprise that the internet knows what you're keen on buying right now. We see this in stalker ads all the time; you search just once for "Cosplay Catsuit", and *bam*! Your feed is full of them.

Oh shucks. Woe is me.

There's another angle, though. More expensive products can absorb a higher CPR.

When I was in the automotive industry (circa 2007ish), Land Rover would pay $15 for a qualified lead. Just a lead! Nothing more than a person who filled out a form who also had the ability to afford a Land Rover.

You can imagine what they would be willing to pay per click to get the *right* person to click on their ad.

You can also imagine the budget they gave the advertisers to play with.

If you give it a moment's thought, you'll realize it's pretty rare to see Facebook ads for a product in the $0 - $7 range. Heck, a pair of half-decent leggings has a better profit margin than our books do.

AVAILABILITY

In short, people on the internet get arranged into a pyramid based on their demographics, economic situation, current needs, and shopping habits.

Here's my super-scientific breakdown:

At the tippity-top of the pyramid are people who are currently in the market for their own tropical island and a Learjet to fly there.

A little further down are folks looking to buy their next house, then a couple of notches below them are Audi shoppers. Next are people buying things like washing machines, then a shiny new iPhone, followed by that Ninja air fryer, a nifty toaster, then the aforementioned leggings.

At the very bottom of the pyramid are people who aren't currently buying anything, or who are not known to click on ads—which makes them of little interest to advertisers.

That razor-thin sliver is *our* part of the audience.

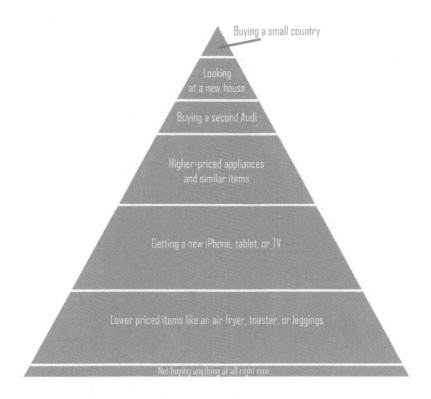

INTEREST LEVEL

But that's just one of the variables. The next is interest level. We all know that there are people who are interested in a given topic, and then there are people who *live for it*.

When we pick interests to build an audience in the Ad Manager, you can bet your bottom dollar that the nice chonky audience size we turn up includes people who showed a passing interest in our selected items a couple years back.

Let's imagine I'm advertising to *Star Wars* fans. Here's how they break down.

At the outer ring are people who maybe watched a movie or two. Next in, we have people who keep up on most of the movies and shows, then folks that *really* soak up pretty much everything *Star Wars*. At the very center are the superfans. These are the people with their own *Star Wars* YouTube channel (I am casting no aspersions. You people rock.)

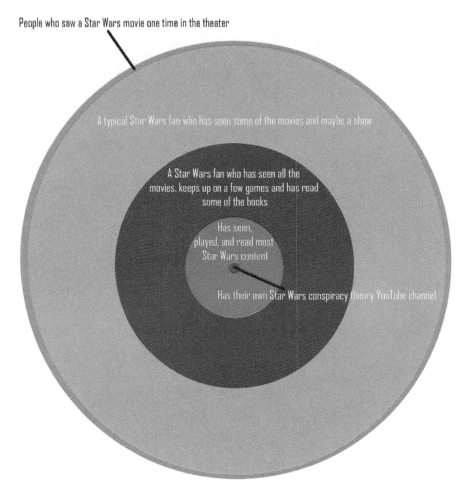

People who saw a Star Wars movie one time in the theater

A typical Star Wars fan who has seen some of the movies and maybe a show

A Star Wars fan who has seen all the movies, keeps up on a few games and has read some of the books

Has seen, played, and read most Star Wars content

Has their own Star Wars conspiracy theory YouTube channel

Some of these people will not be buying much at all right now, and some of them will be buying things that put their CPR out of our range. Here's the combined visual:

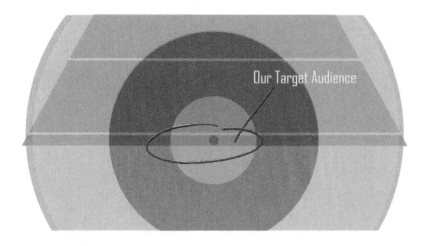

The audience segment where the high-interest people overlap with the folks not buying pricey stuff is our sweet spot. That's where we can get the best CPR and the best Result Rate.

As we increase spend, we start to move out of the center of that target and into groups of people where bidding for our interests will be more competitive, and therefore more expensive. Folks outside of the center will also be less likely to click, which will lower our Result Rate.

This is why I like building audiences of *at least* a million. My goal is to make the number of people in that ideal audience sweet spot as voluminous as possible.

At this point, maybe you've forgotten what the third variable is. Don't worry, I haven't.

AD LEARNING LIMIT

When your ad is first in the learning phase, Facebook casts a wide net, searching for folks who show a keen interest in your ad, and then building a subset of the available audience around that core group.

Essentially, it's figuring out who fits in this center area.

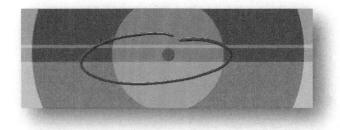

Here's the rub. How wide the system casts that net depends greatly on your budget. A \$5/day ad spend will reach about 750 people during the learning phase. Out of the millions in your total audience size, that's a pretty small sample.

That smaller initial budget can also limit the size of the internal audience that Meta is actually showing your ad to (your maximum Reach).

Now, people naturally filter in and out of this pool as their shopping and interest habits shift. But there does seem to be a ceiling, where scaling up the ad's spend results in more cost and a few more clicks, but not more sales (or at least, not enough to offset the increased ad spend).

This is where you've hit your Learning Limit.

A normal scenario is to bump up the ad spend by about \$5/day every 3-5 days, then wait to see if the CPR, Result Rate, and conversions perform as expected—then do it again.

However, this slow, incremental process does not put the ad back into a learning phase, and thus does not adjust that internal Reach limit that Meta has in mind for your ad.

To break this limit, you need to get the ad back into the learning phase.

There are two ways to do this: adjust your audience, or jack up your ad spend.

Adjusting the audience means adding or eliminating a couple of interests to change up the pool. Jacking up the ad spend means making an increase of over $30 - $50 (depending on what the ad's spend is at the time).

That will force Meta to reevaluate your audience and once again show the ad to a larger pool of people as it builds its new targets.

Yes. This is scary.

SAFELY SCALE AN AD

Let's talk about how to scale an ad without giving yourself an ulcer.

Start an ad at $5/day and tweak it as described in the Analyzing Ads section. Get a good CPR and Result Rate, and start scaling it up by $/5day every 3-5 days, waiting for a bit each time to ensure that the CPR and Result Rate don't go out of bounds. Also keep an eye on the conversions in the Amazon Attribution Tag system.

If it is performing well, bump it up again. You'll likely reach a point of diminishing returns around $20 - $30.

There are two roads forward at this point.

Road one is to drop it down $5 or so, and let the ad run for months and months without worrying about it too much. Rather than take the risk of bumping this ad up to $50 – $100 a day, you can start new ads directed at slightly different audiences, and try to find other subsets of that ideal pool of people.

This is absolutely viable, and the way many people build a stable of well-performing ads that keep their books selling.

The other road is to take the plunge and jack up that ad's spend by a significant amount while keeping a *keen eye* on all the metrics.

It's not a surefire path to success, but when it works, it *works*.

PART 9: ADDITIONAL TIPS AND TWEAKS

A TRICK TO IMPROVE SOCIAL PROOF

As I've mentioned before, you can change the audience on an ad and not remove the likes, shares, or comments on that ad. This means an audience change doesn't lose your social proof.

Something I often do with ads is run them for the first few days targeted at my fans, and friends of my fans. Then, once I get good relevancy/engagement scores, and rack up some comments, likes, and shares, I alter my audience to *exclude* my fans.

This used to be a simple option right below where you make an audience, but now it requires building a custom audience.

To do that, click the "Create New" button above the custom audience box, then select "Custom Audience".

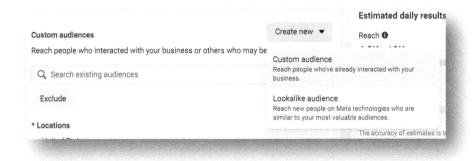

Note: Your version of Ad Manager may look slightly different than this, but there should be similar options in the same location.

A new window will pop up asking for the custom audience source. Choose "Facebook Page", and click Next.

This may not seem immediately intuitive, but all ads run under pages, so interactions on ads count as page interactions.

On the next screen, select your page, and choose "Everyone who engaged with your Page" as the event. Engagement on pages includes page likes and follows, as well as likes, comments, shares, and link clicks on ads.

Give the audience a descriptive name and click "Create Audience".

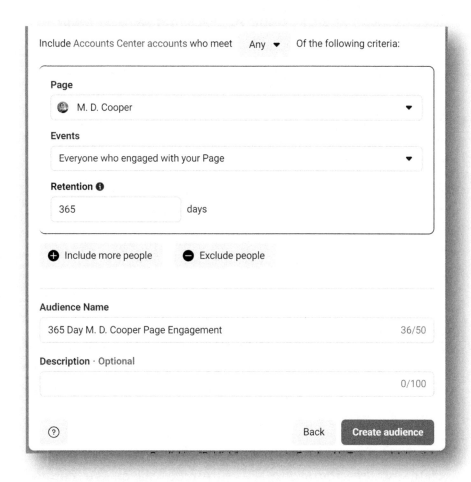

The audience will be created, and a window will pop up asking us what we want to do with the audience. We're already doing it, so we can just close that window.

Note: The page you select should be at least a year old, and you need to have either 1000+ followers on that page or have been running ads for several months at the minimum using that page.

If not, the audience won't be large enough, and the CPR will be very high.

This will take us back to the Ad Set window where our new custom audience will be loaded in.

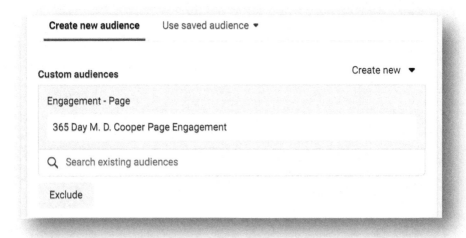

Everyone in this audience is likely already there because we've targeted them with ads or other marketing activities based on their interests. As a result, there is no need to further narrow this audience.

That means you can leave all of the other selections in their default states—though make sure you select the country where you most frequently run your ads, as that is where the bulk of this custom audience will reside.

If, for example, you frequently run ads to both the US and UK, then you could add both countries, though the links you use in your ad will need to work for both locations.

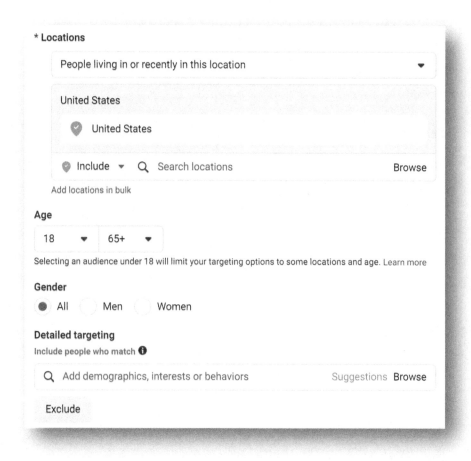

This is the only time I'll suggest targeting more than one country. Normally it will reduce your usable audience too much, but in this case it won't.

Because this audience will likely be numbered in the thousands, not millions, it won't last for long, probably only five days or so. It may also have a higher CPR. You'll need to keep an eye on it.

Once you've garnered some social proof on the ad, it's time to flip the script!

Edit the Ad Set and go to the audience section. Mouse over the custom audience to show a little down arrow. Click it, and select "Exclude".

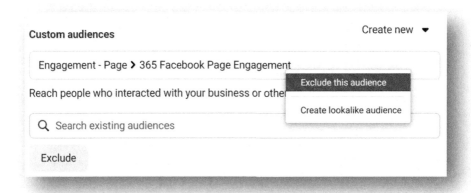

This will move our page engagement audience to the excluded section. This will move it down to a new section, and leave the "Include" section blank.

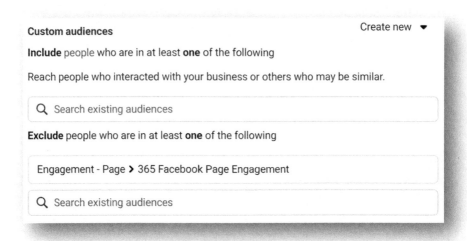

Once that is done. build an audience normally using the country, age, gender, and interests that are appropriate.

The social proof on the ad will remain and we can now show the ad to an entirely new group of people.

ADVANTAGE CUSTOM AUDIENCES

Facebook has recently added a new option for custom audiences called "Advantage custom audience". This appears to be an automatic lookalike audience that is layered on top of your custom audience.

Depending on the size of your custom audience and your goals, this may be useful, but in this case it isn't—as it runs contrary to the entire purpose of this exercise.

Advantage custom audience ✦
✓ Reach people beyond your custom audience when it is likely to improve performance.

AD COMMENTS

Where I first spoke about social proof, I mentioned that Facebook by and large considers all comments to be good comments. A healthy debate between two people (even if there is negativity and disagreement) is good business when your product is the discourse.

To that end, even "This book sucks poo poo" is a comment that boosts social proof. That being said, you really don't want that on your ad, do you?

What I do with comments like that is hide them, and let them live in their little echo chamber. Sometimes I hide them but still respond, if the comment isn't too antagonistic.

However, just like you need a few 1-3-star reviews of your book, some lemon comments don't really hurt much, either. In fact, they may help.

In the past I've run a challenge ad where I ask, "Is M. D. Cooper the next Larry Niven?" (For non-SF nerds, Larry Niven has been a Science Fiction titan since the early 70s).

That's a pretty tall order. I don't think I'm as good as Larry Niven, even on my best day. However, it has sparked some fun comments.

Some I've hidden, but others I've engaged with, and we've discussed the merits of his books and mine. Some comments had people saying that his stuff sucked and mine was great.

That being said, don't run challenge ads under your own Facebook author page. Those need to live under one of your fan/genre pages so that you can address the comments with your marketing/publicist hat on.

Also, just like 1-star reviews (yes, I respond to many of those, too), if the posted comment has burned your cookies, let it sit for a day and see if it still bugs you enough to reply to it.

Whatever you do, don't get upset with folks. Your readers are seeing your ads too, and they won't be happy if you behave like an ass.

PRODUCT PAGE TWEAKS

This is a final little note that may help your product page convert just a bit better.

You're bound to have a particular ad that is your *main* ad at any given time. It may be character, plot, or even deal related. But you want that ad to have a good flow into your product page so that the reader feels continuity.

To that end, I recommend you add a bit of text at the top of your blurb that connects it to your ad.

For example, my book blurbs are almost always character-based (talking about my main character and her challenges), but my best performing ad was plot-based, so the first paragraph of the blurb bore little resemblance to the ad.

To remedy this, I added in a bold paragraph that was a good grab line, and also connected to the ad.

This one change boosted my ad's conversion rate by 20%.

THE DEATH OF YOUR AD

All good ads go to heaven, so it's OK to kill that ad when its relevancy/engagement wanes, its CPR starts to climb, or its result rate diminishes.

I suspect you won't have too much trouble killing off dead ads, since they hit you in the wallet. However, those ads that ran long and did well can have a second life.

Take a look at the demographics you selected (be it gender, country, or age), and see if you can tweak the ad and give it new life by hitting a new demographic.

I recently had an ad that ran from November to May, and was finally getting to the end of its life. However, I looked at it and saw that I had made a silly mistake that caused it to have never shown in the UK.

The mistake: I used a lookalike audience that was US-only as the foundation of the Ad Set audience.

Well, well, well, I thought to myself, as I rubbed my hands together and quickly duplicated that ad with a UK-only target. Sure enough, there was this massive group of people across the pond that loved my ad.

That book has since moved from an average ranking of 12,000 in the UK store to about 2500 as a result.

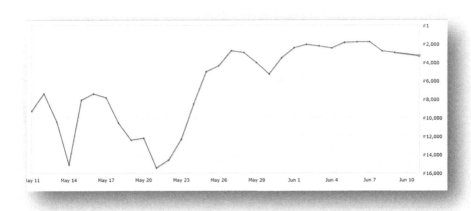

UK Sales Rank over the month. Down a bit now, which means I need to look at my audience saturation, but it's quite the jump!

That one little glance at a dying ad put a 5-year-old book into the top 2000 in the UK store.

Another option (which I also undertook) to give a plot-based ad new life is to retool its copy to be more character-based. The ad I applied this method to had previously bombed with women, but with retooling, it did well (not amazing, but well) among that group, and has probably sold about 400 books at this point.

GET THAT AD DOING DOUBLE DUTY

While the standard creation process has you make new ads to put in Ad Sets, you can also take existing ads and put them into a *second* Ad Set.

NOTE: This technique does not work with Dynamic Creative

What this means is you can have a single ad that you show to men, women, USA, and UK, but rather than lumping all those demographics into one audience, you can make multiple Ad Sets to capture those audiences with different budgets while serving them the same ad.

This is a great way to take an ad that's working well and has good social proof, and leverage it further.

To do this, choose the "Use Existing Post" option when creating an ad.

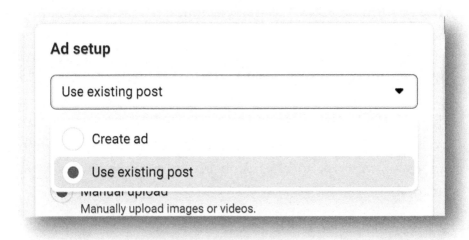

Then scroll down to the Ad Creative section and click "Select Post". On the next screen, you can pick the ad, or even a post from your page that you wish to use.

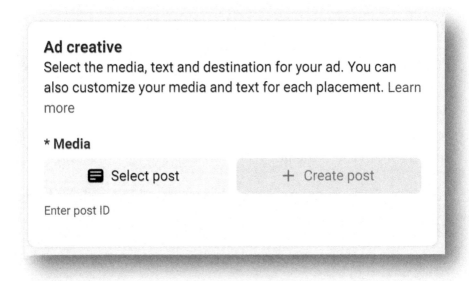

Once you select the content, the existing creative (image, text, etc) will be applied, along with the social proof.

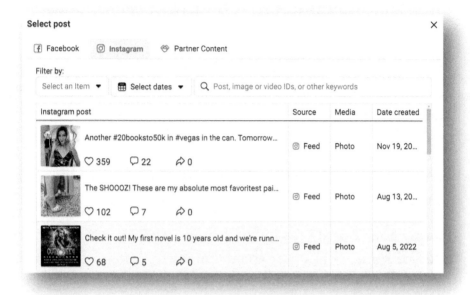

Remember, in this case, it's not a *new* ad; it's two Ad Sets using the same existing ad (or an ad using an actual post from your page or Instagram). So if you change something on the original, the copy in the new Ad will be edited as well.

PART 10: VIDEO ADS

Video ads on Facebook have two purposes: prompting direct action (sending people to buy your book), and building an audience of people who engage with your content.

MAKING YOUR OWN VIDEO WITH FACEBOOK'S TOOLS

Shortly after I wrote the initial version of this book, Facebook released some tools a user could employ to dynamically make their own videos out of static images.

Frankly, they sucked.

However, they've really come a long way. Now you can upload up to six images, and the video creation tool will give you a number of options, some even seasonally festive.

To begin, click the "Create Video" button on the ad creation page.

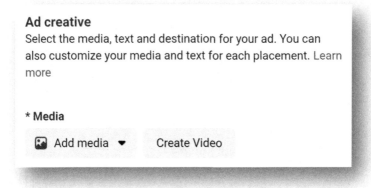

Once the new window opens, you can upload up to *fifteen* images to create a variety of videos with custom text overlays.

There are three templates. One to make square videos), one for vertical, and one flexible template that can work for multiple placements.

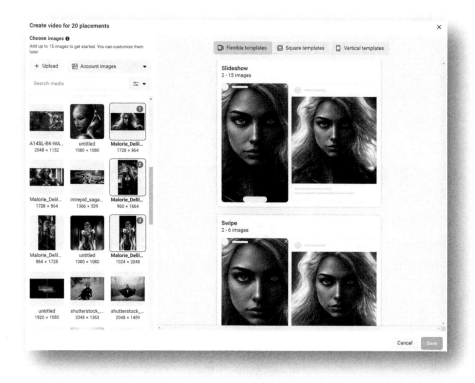

You'll want to click "Save" (at least, I always do), but it's disabled. To proceed, click "Edit" on your preferred option to create a video in that style. The next page will allow you to alter the order of images, add stickers, change transitions, and manage a few other settings.

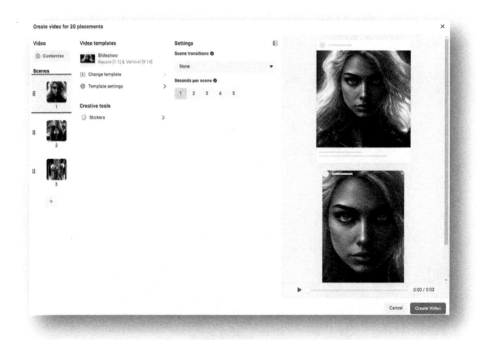

In effect, what you're doing is creating a better-than-average slideshow. One would think they couldn't be effective, but often these simple slideshows work better than custom-made videos.

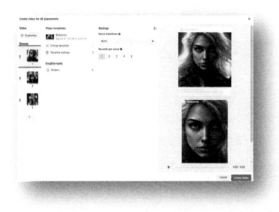

To customize each image in the slide, click it, then choose crop, text overlay, or logo.

The text overlay options are quite robust and make it possible to tell a story with your images.

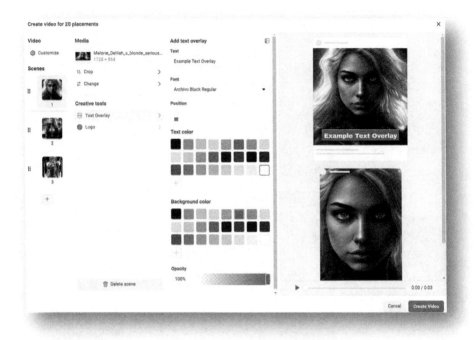

To go back to the prior screen, click "Customize" in the upper left corner. This is where you can play through the video and customize the length of time each image shows as well as the scene transitions.

Once you're satisfied, you can create your video by pressing the blue "Create Video" button in the lower right. The process will take a minute or two to complete.

If you are using Dynamic Creative, this video will be added to your pool of images and videos. If you are not using DC, then it will become the single visual creative your ad serves.

The following image shows scenes from a video I created in couple minutes with images I'd uploaded for previous ads.

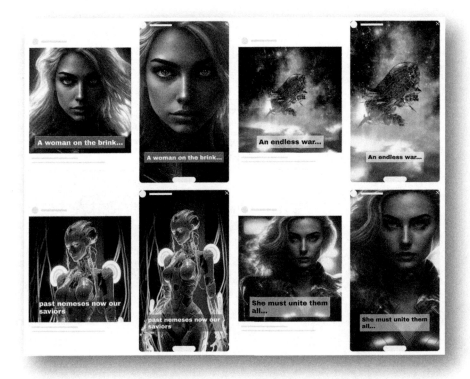

OTHER VIDEO TOOLS

There are a host of programs and web platforms out there that you can use to make videos. From the top-of-the-line Adobe Premiere Pro, to more affordable (and easier to use) tools like Movavi (a personal favorite) ,or Apple's movie editor.

Online tools such as Book Brush and Canva can also make good videos.

A HANDY WORKAROUND

I'm sure you haven't forgotten the conundrum that Facebook's dislike of text on ads creates. Well, video is a handy workaround. There is no penalty for putting text on a video ad, nor any issue with putting your book cover in there.

With video, you can have your cake and eat it too.

Start off with compelling scenes that will grab the viewer's attention, and then show your book cover to make it plain as day that the ad is for a book.

Voila! Problem solved.

LENGTH MATTERS

Just not the way you might think.

Facebook used to recommend that videos stay under 45 seconds, but now they recommend that they are under 15 seconds. The reason for this is twofold.

1. People have short attention spans. So be concise. Your video should only have one sentence in it. The video above contains this: "In the year 4123, Major Tanis Richards has one job: get the ship Outsystem."

2. Until the video finishes playing, clicking on it only pauses the playback. Once it's done, this overlay appears:

Download
www.amazon.com

You don't want someone to have to wait 45 seconds to see the prompt to download. Yes, it is also in the CTA box below the ad image, but the more access the user has to it, the better.

As you know, I also recommend adding a text link in the description above the ad image. That way, there are two prompts: one above the video, and one below, should they choose to click while the video is still playing.

LOWER CPR AHEAD

What you are likely to find is that video ads get a low CPR. This is because Facebook *likes* video, and because there is less on the platform. They have made a lot of tools for turning still images into videos, and the result can work as well as a real video, provided it's done well.

Keep in mind that a good custom video (using software rather than an online tool) with compelling graphics and good music can cost you $50 – $100—on the low end. This is why I recommend not experimenting with video ads until you really have still-image ads nailed.

There is, however, an exception to this rule. I mean...there always is, right?

USE YOUR WORDS

Literally...

Something I have had moderate success with, and other authors have had great success with, is doing readings as video ads.

If you do a non-scheduled FB Live video, or upload a video of your own making, you can convert them into ads; some people have had great success doing this.

Now, this depends a lot on how good a reading you can do, and whether you are comfortable being in front of the camera—quiet environment, etc....

PART 11: BOOSTED POSTS

It would be remiss of me not to discuss boosted posts, as they are a great way to engage with your readers. But they are less effective at general advertising.

There's a reason for this: they're not traffic ads, they're engagement ads.

Facebook is not seeking out folks who are likely to click the link, they're hunting for folks who will engage in *any* way.

These ads often have *very low* CPR, because the R (result) in that acronym is not a click, it's any activity at all!

This does make them great for reaching out to your readers when you want them to know about new books coming out, current deals or promotions, upcoming books, etc...

So *do* use them when you want to interact with your existing audience, but *don't* use them when you are trying to sell books to a new set of readers.

GO FORTH AND CREATE!

You are now imbued with the knowledge to create ads and determine if they're working.

Remember: your book, audience, ad copy, cover, blurb, and the story itself are entirely unique to you. What works for someone else may not work for you.

There are no silver bullets

The name of the game is trial and testing. There's no alchemy involved. Basic math and measuring effectiveness of ads (while only making incremental changes to variables) is the method wherein you will find successful ads and scale them.

That being said, there is an art to this process. Just like you didn't become a proficient writer overnight, it will take time to master creating and refining ads. Don't despair if you don't get home runs every time.

Lastly, if you need help, we are here. We at the Writing Wives often hosts webinars and courses specifically aimed at helping authors master ads, as well as one-on-one training that will assist you in leveling up your ad game.

AN OFFER FROM THE WRITING WIVES

The information contained within this book is the foundation of what any author needs to know in order to take their book sales to the next level.

However, every combination of book, cover, title, blurb, genre, tropes, story, and author, is unique. While the advice in these pages is accurate and actionable, it's not personalized to your unique situation.

If you're interested in either 1 on 1 coaching, or group class settings where we cover a host of topics and help authors improve their ads and sales, then we'd love to work with you.

A great way to start is to fill out our ad score card and see where yours stand!

Fill out the Ad Scorecard

(https://www.thewritingwives.com/free-fb-ad-scorecard)

You can also reach out to us at jill@thewritingwives.com or malorie@thewritingwives.com.

NON-FICTION BOOKS BY JILL & MALORIE

HELP! I'M AN AUTHOR SERIES

Help! My Facebook Ads Suck *Third Edition*

Help! My Launch Plan Sucks

Help! My Blurbs and Ad Copy Suck

Look for these and other **Help, I'm an Author!** books coming soon at www.thewritingwives.com/our-books

GLOSSARY

Yes, boring...but necessary. I want to get a few of these terms defined and out of the way, so that when we get into the meat, you'll know what they mean.

CONVERSION

This one is simple. It is the rate at which someone who lands on a page or sees an ad performs the desired action.

If it's an ad, then the conversion action is the click-through. If it's your book's page on a retailer site (like Amazon), then it's the user clicking the glorious orange "Buy" button.

CPC (Cost per Click)

The CPC of an ad is how much (on average) you pay for a viewer to click the CTA (or any other link) on your ad.

Facebook has a number of CPC metrics, but the one you'll want to pay most attention to is the CPR (cost per result).

CPM (Cost per Mil)

This is the cost per thousand (not million) impressions on your ad. I recommend that you pay per click, not by CPM, making this a metric you can view on your ad, but not one that has much meaning here.

CPR (Cost per Result)

The CPR is how much (on average) you pay for a viewer to click the CTA (or any other link) on your ad.

This is the ideal metric to track, because it is the one that Facebook charges us for. It removes duplicate clicks, and doesn't count clicks to profiles and other destinations.

CTA (Call to Action)

A call to action is the thing that says "Hey, Click Here", or "Yo! Do This Thing!" on your ad or page. It's the "Learn more" or "Like" button on an ad, or the "Buy" button on a page.

Any good promotion (even a flyer a random person hands to you on the street) will have a call to action; something they hope you will do.

When the CTA is clicked or followed or taken, that is success.

FUNNEL

Any time there are sales, there is a sales funnel. This is the number of steps it takes to get a customer (in our case, a reader) from first awareness of us as authors, down to the final sale.

Ideally, your funnel should have as few steps as you can get away with. More complex products require longer funnels, but that typically doesn't apply to books.

KU "FULL READ"

When I use this term, I am applying it to the full read conversion of a book in KU. That is to say, if the book has 100 KENP, and you get 95-100 KENP pages read, we assume that is a full read.

Could it be two people reading 50 pages? Certainly; but when we're looking at read-through across multiple books, it's safe to assume that someone who read book 3 also read all of books 2 and 1, so the math works out the same.

IMPRESSION

Impressions are, quite simply, human eyeballs looking at a page or ad.

PRODUCT PAGE

Though I speak mostly about Amazon, the techniques in this book apply to all retailers. The product page is the sell page for your book; if there is a button that starts the process of taking someone's money in exchange for your book, that's the product page. For most of us, this will be our book's listing page on Amazon.

READ-THROUGH/SELL-THROUGH

The percentage of people who read-through one book and go on to the next, or read-through your entire series.

CUMULATIVE READ-THROUGH

This refers specifically to the people who read-through from the first book to a given book in your series (typically to the end, if it's used without specifying a book number).

BOOK-OVER-BOOK READ-THROUGH

The read-through from one specific book in your series to the one immediately following.

ROI

This stands for Return on Investment. Ads are investments, and you want a good return on them. Your ROI is the dollar amount, or percentage, that you make back after spending money on ads.

TRAFFIC

On the internet, "Traffic" is typically synonymous with people's eyeballs looking at a page. In the context of Facebook ads, it means the type of ad that drives traffic to a page somewhere on the web (typically, your Amazon product page).

WIDE

An eBook being "wide" means that it is being sold on more sites than just Amazon, as in a *wide* number of distribution channels.

THANK YOU

Thanks for taking the time to read this book. We really do hope it helps you out on your journey as an author.

As you all know, reviews are the best social proof a book can have, and we would greatly appreciate your review on this one.

The Writing Wives,
Jill & Malorie Cooper

Printed in Great Britain
by Amazon

24533536R00119